Jury of My Peers

Jury of My Peers

A Surgeon's Encounter

with the

Malpractice Crisis

by

Howard C. Snider, Jr., M.D.

Fountain Press
Montgomery, Alabama

ISBN 0-9622607-0-3

To Pam

CONTENTS

Foreword

The quotations, otherwise undocumented, used in this book were taken directly from the court reporters' transcripts of the depositions and the trial. For the most part, they are verbatim as they appeared in those transcripts. A minimal amount of editing was done only where necessary to facilitate the ease of reading. No changes were made which would significantly alter the content or tone of the quotations and proceedings.

Only the name of our patient was changed. The others are all real. I have attempted to be as accurate and as fair as possible in recording the events and the people involved, as well as my observations of them. Although my thoughts were not always flattering to the various characters, the polemic nature of the book compelled me to share them honestly. My descriptions of the people involved reflect only my opinions as they pertain to this particular case and should in no way be construed as an indictment of their capabilities.

Acknowledgements

The constraints of time and space preclude an adequate acknowledgement to all of the many people who have contributed to making this book possible, but I would like to mention a few. It could not have been written without the cooperation of Judge Charles Price, Charlie Stakely, Tommy Keene, Dr. and Mrs. B. F. Dorrough, Dr. Ruth Nabors, Dr. and Mrs. Allan Cheek, and many of the jurors from our trial. I appreciate the time they all devoted and their openness in sharing their thoughts with me.

I am grateful to Paul Woosley for introducing me to the word processor and for being patient with me as I learned to use it. Thanks to Tom Donald for the numerous times, usually on Sunday afternoons, when he unsnarled the seemingly hopeless chaos I had created with his software. Thanks to Margaret O'Neil, Nancy Mayer, Mabel Royal, and especially Joan Embry for helping me print and organize numerous copies of the manuscript.

I am deeply indebted to Bob Bender for reading my early draft and offering many valuable suggestions, and to Fred Braswell for reading and offering advice on a later one. I am grateful to Philip Gidiere for reading the final version and contributing his valuable advice. Special thanks is due to my sister, Martha Pierson, for her expert editorial assistance.

I would be remiss if I did not thank Paul and Camille Butrus and Frank O'Neil for their help. I am particularly grateful to William McDonald for his gracious devotion of time, energy, and expertise in helping me get the book published.

Finally, I am grateful to my wife, Pam, for tolerating my obsession with the book, for always encouraging me, and most of all, for being willing to become a widow to a word processor for such a long period of time.

Chapter 1

Tuesday, August 27, 1985

> *There was never yet a truly great man
> that was not at the same time truly virtuous.*
> —Benjamin Franklin

he quiet stillness of the early August morning stood in stark contrast to the turmoil within me. I envied *Baby Doll*, our four-month-old Boston terrier, as she sniffed the ground in the flower bed on our front lawn. Her greatest concern at the moment was to find the most appropriate spot to relieve herself. It was four a.m. that Tuesday, the second day of the trial. In a few short hours I was to take the witness stand to defend myself against charges of negligence.

I had grossly underestimated the toll that the malpractice suit would eventually take on me. My last full night of sleep was only a faint memory from the past. I resembled a survivor from Auschwitz, as my normally slender six-foot frame had deteriorated to a gaunt 145 pounds. It felt as though a fire had been raging in my stomach, and it continued to smoulder despite generous doses of *Mylanta* and *Tagamet*.

As I sat in a rocking chair on our front patio, I made a mental note to call my office later that morning to make arrangements for one of my partners in our six-man surgical group in Montgomery, Alabama, to take my regularly scheduled night call on Thursday. Only a few weeks earlier I had naively told our office manager that the trial would be only in daytime hours so I could take my regular night call during the week. I must have been suffering from a mild form of madness when I made that assessment. There was no way I was physically or emotionally able to take care of patients that week.

The front door opened and Pam peered out, her hair disheveled and her eyes bleary. I could tell that the stress was beginning to take its toll on her as well. She had worked feverishly over the weekend to complete a take-home final exam in her doctoral program in counseling so that she could be available day and night to support me during my week of agony. I wondered silently if we would feel like celebrating our first wedding anniversary in a couple of weeks.

Baby Doll romped over and leaped wildly to kiss Pam as she made her way to sit in the rocking chair next to me.

"It's a little early, isn't it?" Pam asked.

"Yeah, but I just couldn't sleep. I want to be so prepared for anything Hogan brings up that there is no way he can trap me into saying something I don't mean. I'm just sort of going over things in my mind."

"How long have you been awake?" asked Pam.

"Awake? All night. Out here? Fifteen minutes."

"Why don't we go inside? I'll make some coffee, then I'll be the jury and listen to what you are going to say," Pam offered.

"I think that might help a lot," I said as we walked inside. "Sometimes I use words that I have become so familiar with over the last twenty years I can't remember whether non-medical people know what they mean or not."

It had been almost twenty-one years since I walked up the steps of the Basic Science Building to begin my freshman year at the Medical College of Alabama in Birmingham. I was twenty-one years old that crisp September morning in 1964, and very naive. I had no inkling then that one day *I* would have to face my accusers and answer charges of medical malpractice. The very words connoted something synonymous with a bad doctor, derelict in his duty, wantonly and negligently harming patients through ignorance or callousness. The thought never crossed my mind that I could study diligently and practice conscientiously, yet still be accused of malpractice.

At the very core of my being there has always been an innate drive to do well in whatever endeavor I undertook — to excel. As a result, I studied awfully hard in medical school and burned the midnight oil many a Saturday night when others were sleeping or partying. This desire for excellence was tremendously enhanced during my senior year in medical school when I spent my surgical rotation with Dr. John Kirklin, the Chief of Surgery at University Hospital, a brilliant person and an eminent surgical scholar of world renown. No one I have ever known approaches his singular dedication to excellence in everything he does. I shall never forget the exhilaration I felt when he called me aside at the end of my student rotation with him, complimented me on the work that I had done, and offered to help me in any way he could in the future. His recommendation, coupled with a number two rank in my graduating class, enabled me to do my internship at The Johns Hopkins Hospital, a prestigious, but rigorous program which provided an incredible amount of experience.

Following my internship, I returned to Birmingham and spent four years in a surgical residency under Dr. Kirklin, one of the best surgical educators in the world. My admiration for him increased with the passing years and, with it, my desire to emulate his excellence. There were numerous occasions when something he said or did would impact upon me in a very special way, but one occasion stands out particularly in my memory. I was making rounds with him on Christmas Eve — one of those rare times when there was not an entourage of students and residents — just the two of us. We were standing in the intensive care unit at the foot of the bed of a young mathematics professor from North Carolina. The professor had come to Birmingham, as people did from all over the world, because he wanted to have his heart repaired by the very best. Tragically, a complication had developed during cardiopulmonary bypass, and the pump had filled his brain with clots. His brain was dead, and it was only a matter of time before his heart would stop beating. His wife sat all alone in an otherwise deserted waiting room, maintaining her lonely vigil far from home, awaiting the inevitable. To this day I am not certain what prompted it — perhaps Dr. Kirklin sensed the compassion I was feeling for this man and his family — but he turned to me and, quite unexpectedly said, "Howard, you're going to be great." It was for me a profound experience. My heart was burdened with sadness because of the tragic situation but, at the same time filled with joy that this great man, who had received virtually every accolade a surgeon could receive, was telling *me* that *I* was going to be great.

I suppose it is human nature to try to live up to the expectations of those whom we admire. Although I have fallen far short of the excellence necessary to be recognized as "great," I have never stopped trying, particularly in my attempts to always do what is right, and just, and compassionate. Dr. Kirklin had many admonitions for us, but the one I have perhaps come closest to fulfilling was his noble exhortation "to do your level best for every patient, regardless of who he is, who is watching, or how much he can pay."

It's not easy — this business of being a doctor — entrusted on a daily basis with people's very lives. It demands much soul-searching, often done in the wee hours of the night, when others are sleeping peacefully. It is not easy to sleep at night when your days are filled with death or the threat of death. What person, if involved in the death of another — in an automobile accident, or a hunting accident, or perhaps just as a passerby at the moment of death — could sleep placidly without second guessing his every action? What if I had turned down a different street? Should I have been going slower? Could some quick action on my part have saved the life?

For a physician involved in caring for critically ill patients, this process of self analysis and criticism is unending, not only for deaths, but for every complication, every bad result. Too numerous to count are the nights each year that I lie awake staring at my bedroom ceiling, alone in the recesses of my mind, thinking, wondering, analyzing, reflecting. Through the years, I have been my own harshest critic, judging myself by a standard of perfection unattainable to mortals. Thus, a charge of negligence — malpractice — leveled against me by others, when I judged the care I had rendered the patient as close to perfect as I could attain, struck at the very core of my being.

Chapter 2

What deep wounds ever closed
without a scar?
—Byron

Although I had been vaguely aware for years that a malpractice trial causes great emotional strain on physicians, I was totally unaware of the depths of the emotional upheaval wrought by such an experience until I faced it myself. The experience is deep, personal, and profound. The myriad of feelings is almost universal — the initial embarrassment, followed by frustration, bewilderment, and ultimately anger. One of the only positive aspects of my ordeal was that it gave me greater empathy for my colleagues who have suffered similar fates.

In any aspect of life, the deeper a person's commitment to an ideal, or a person, or a profession, the greater that person's vulnerability when that commitment is assailed. The price one pays for caring deeply is the ever-present potential for being hurt equally as deeply. So it is in medicine. The most conscientious, caring physicians are often the ones who seem to suffer the most as a result of lawsuits.

No one that I know was any more devastated by a malpractice lawsuit than Ruth Nabors, a charming person and an excellent anesthesiologist. Normally possessed with serene, unshakable composure, there were times during her ordeal when she bordered on becoming completely unglued.

Ruth's initial encounter with her plaintiff was on preoperative rounds the night before a proposed cataract operation. The patient was particularly anxious, so Ruth spent a great deal of time with her, carefully explaining the risks of anesthesia, patiently answering questions, and allaying fears. Unfortunately, the agent she gave to induce anesthesia the following day caused the bronchial tubes in the patient's lungs to go into spasm, making it unsafe to proceed with the operation and necessitating the abortion of the procedure. The spasm was so severe that the patient had to be treated with a respirator for several days, but no permanent damage was done.

Ruth agonized during the hospitalization, distraught that a patient of hers had a serious complication. She visited at length with the family, desperately needing them to tell her it was okay — that they understood things like this happen. Instead, they were overtly hostile toward her from the start, blaming her for the complication and giving her the distinct impression that she would be sued. Several weeks after being discharged from the hospital, the patient and her family approached the ophthalmologist with a deal. If he would just testify that Ruth had somehow done something wrong, they would not name him in their lawsuit. Since he did not believe anyone had done anything wrong, he refused their request, was subsequently named in the suit also, and endured it to the bitter end. The major contention of the suit was that the patient had sustained mental anguish from the ordeal and, consequently, would never be able to endure the stress of having the operation for her cataract. She weakened her case considerably by having a successful cataract operation before the trial took place.

Ruth was embarrassed to have a lawsuit filed against her. She tried desperately to get her attorney and her insurance company to settle the case and avoid the publicity and emotional strain of a trial. However, they did not believe she had done anything which would justify that approach and could not accommodate Ruth's personal desires. The realization that she had no control over the situation and would be forced to go to court almost wrecked her. She withdrew into a protective shell, isolating herself emotionally from her friends and her family. She would not discuss the case with her closest friends, and her parents did not even find out about the suit until shortly before the trial date. She began to resent her attorney-husband for being a part of the legal system which seemed to be torturing her. His attempts to help her by telling her not to take things so personally only made matters worse. She became such an emotional wreck that he had to literally hide any mail pertaining to the suit until he could get her into a good enough frame of mind to handle it without going to pieces.

Ruth had trouble cooperating with her attorney because she resented the legal game he was asking her to play. She wanted to just tell her story and let the facts speak for them-

selves. Instead, she was asked to look up obscure minutiae
in the literature to substantiate points which seemed irrelevant to her. From her perspective, they were straying further
and further away from the important facts in the case in
order to have a nice story for the jury. Whereas the case they
were building was true, it had little to do with what was
medically important; but it was what would win with an
uneducated jury.

When the trial began, the plaintiff's attorneys portrayed
Ruth as an incompetent anesthesiologist who had been fired
from her job at Baptist Medical Center. Nothing could have
been further from the truth. The jurors had little trouble
in seeing where the truth lay, deliberating only seven minutes
before reaching a verdict for the defendants; but the lies and
innuendos had wounded her deeply. After the verdict was
returned, a female attorney who had been representing the
plaintiff came up to Ruth and told her she hoped she knew
that this had not been anything personal. Ruth, ordinarily
the epitome of Southern charm and sweetness, looked her
in the eye and said, "Please go straight to Hell. I'm sorry,
but I hate you so much. You just don't know how much I
hate you."

Ruth now practices in fear with the knowledge that lurk-
ing out there somewhere is a child who will react to an anesthetic and die. If she puts enough people to sleep, it will
eventually happen; and conscientious, careful practice will
not be able to prevent it. Each morning she asks herself if
this is the day something bad will happen. The emotional
devastation she felt with her first suit pales when she contemplates what she would experience if a child died and the
parents blamed her.

Though she loves practicing anesthesiology, if she could
find any profession nearly as enjoyable, she would quit to-

day. It is easy to understand why she says that if she had it to do over again, she would not go to medical school.

Malpractice lawsuits have a way of transforming physicians who, by nature, are relaxed, compassionate, and trusting into fearful people who harbor resentment and are distrustful of their patients. Allan Cheek is a neonatologist — a good one. On a daily basis he treats high-risk premature babies as they struggle for life. He, also, lives in perpetual fear of his next lawsuit and resents the ordeal he went through as a result of trying his level best to do what was right, and caring, and kind.

Allan and his partners (he was in a group at the time) accepted in transfer from another hospital a very high-risk baby with severe birth-related brain damage. The parents were already angry at their obstetrician and at the hospital where the delivery had taken place and had retained a lawyer to investigate the possibility of filing suit for what they perceived to be poor care. This combination of a high risk infant and angry, litigious parents portended possible trouble. The neonatologists could have refused to accept this legal powder keg, but they agreed to care for him. Cognizant that there could be legal problems down the road, they were careful from the outset to do everything just right.

It soon became apparent that the baby's brain damage was so severe and his coma so deep that his chance for survival was almost nil. The possibility of discontinuing the respirator in the event of brain death was discussed with the parents. However, to the surprise of the physicians, the infant continued to show some brain activity on his electroencephalogram and, therefore, did not meet the criteria for being brain-dead. Though the odds were low, there was a slim chance the baby could improve and survive. A pediatric neurologist was called in, and he confirmed the opinion that the baby was severely, and almost hopelessly brain damaged, but not brain-dead. Since there were reports in the literature of babies being in comas for months before coming out of them, the physicians could not discontinue the respirator unless the baby developed brain death.

Because of the dismal outlook for the baby, the parents decided they wanted the respirator to be discontinued anyway, a request which left the doctors in a quandary. They understood the parents' reasoning and wanted to help them, but they did not believe they could withdraw care from an infant who was not brain-dead. A short time earlier, two physicians in California had been indicted for murder when they, at the family's request, withdrew treatment from a hopelessly ill patient. Also, the Reagan administration had issued the controversial Baby Doe regulations, threatening prosecution to any physician who withheld care from any infant, regardless of the severity of the brain damage. There was a hot-line, toll-free number to Washington posted in every neonatal care unit in the country inviting a call from anyone who suspected care was being withheld from any baby. It seemed out of the question for the physicians to remove the respirator and allow the baby to die. The hospital lawyer was consulted and confirmed that, without a court order, the respirator could not be removed. The hospital chaplain was called in to counsel the parents. He and the doctors helped the parents file a petition with the family court requesting that the respirator be removed. The judge refused to rule in the case, claiming it was a medical and not a legal problem, leaving everyone in limbo. After languishing for several months, the baby finally died. During the time the baby lingered, the parents' hostility gradually shifted from the original hospital and doctor to the hospital and doctors who could not allow their baby to die. After the baby died, suit was filed against the hospital and doctors charging malpractice as it relates to the definition of death in Alabama, assault and battery of a minor with a deadly weapon (the respirator), fraud, and "outrage." Everyone scoffed at the frivolous nature of the charges and assumed the nuisance suit would eventually be dropped; but it was not.

The suit made a nightmare out of what otherwise would have been just a difficult time in Allan's life. He had separated from his group under rather unfriendly circumstances and had nobody who could share call with him. By the time the case came to trial, he was exhausted from two years of constant work. He was having bouts of severe pain from a diseased gallbladder but could not arrange coverage for his practice in order to have the needed operation. He did not have the time or energy he needed to devote to his children, and they were beginning to suffer as a result. They were also asking why their father was being sued for being a bad doctor. His mother suffered a stroke a month or two before the trial, adding to his worries. The crowning blow, though, came several weeks before the trial began. The county sheriff served him notice that his former partners, who were on trial with him and would be sitting in the courtroom beside him, were suing him over a monetary dispute relating to his former practice.

Allan's problems were compounded by the fact that he had to get a neonatologist from another city to come to Montgomery and cover his practice while he was sitting at the courthouse — and sit at the courthouse he did. The marathon trial began two weeks before Christmas, recessed for the holidays, then lasted until the third week in January. Allan was on the witness stand two full days, one of which found him suffering from the effects of a severe intestinal virus. The plaintiff's attorney harassed him on the stand to the point that the judge had to threaten him with contempt of court to get him to stop.

When the long ordeal ended, and the jury returned a verdict for the defendants, Allan was so physically and emotionally depleted that he could not even celebrate. He just dragged himself back to work. He wonders how much longer he can continue to take care of high-risk babies. At least once a month he gets a notice that another of his charts has been subpoenaed by a plaintiff's attorney for review. The less risky life of a general pediatrician appeals more to him with each passing day.

Physicians who deliver babies and care for newborns are the targets of a large percentage of malpractice lawsuits. Certainly this skewed distribution does not relate to the doctors' degree of competence. It results from the fact that juries are naturally sympathetic toward parents whose babies are less than perfect. In addition, when one multiplies the projected life expectancy of the infants by a large amount of money for care per year, the result is astronomical, attracting the attention of plaintiffs' attorneys.

Probably one of the most unjust lawsuits anywhere was filed against one of Montgomery's most dedicated and beloved physicians. Dr. Bernie Dorrough devoted much of his life to faithfully serving the citizens of the community, delivering over 10,000 babies in his forty years of practice. Toward the end of his career, he was aware that obstetrics had become a high risk area for lawsuits. However, he conscientiously kept up with the latest developments in the field and felt comfortable in his belief that, if he spent time with his patients, related well to them, and did a good job in caring for them, he would never be sued. He didn't count on the vindictiveness of one of his patients who got a "bad" baby.

The ill-fated patient called Dr. Dorrough after midnight at the end of an uncomplicated, full-term pregnancy telling him that her membranes had ruptured. He advised her to go to the hospital immediately, then called the labor room and asked them to check her as soon as she arrived and call him when they had finished. Upon arriving at the hospital, the patient was examined by the labor room nurse in charge, who determined that she was in very early labor with an undilated cervix and ruptured membranes. Dr. Dorrough was called at home and gave the routine orders that had served him so well over the previous thirty-five years. The patient was connected very briefly to the fetal monitor, an instrument which detects distress of the baby during labor. The strip appeared to be completely normal, so the patient was disconnected and the standard obstetrical preparations were begun. After the prep was completed, the patient was again connected to the fetal monitor. This time the nurses noted some changes on the monitor strip which concerned them. They called Dr. Dorrough, who dressed immediately and arrived at the hospital seventeen minutes later. After looking at the strip, he felt it was unwise to attempt natural delivery and scheduled an immediate Caesarean section, delivering the baby within thirty minutes after his arrival. The baby was flaccid and unresponsive at delivery with a zero Apgar; but after ten minutes of resuscitation by a second obstetrician who assisted with the delivery, the baby's Apgar was one. The infant was noted to have multiple deformities which appeared to be genetic in nature. (Photographs of the infant's deformities were later shown to the jury). During the weeks the baby was in the Neonatal Intensive Care Unit, the neonatologist attempted to get the parents to have genetic testing performed both on the infant and on themselves, but they refused. After being hospitalized with essentially no change and no physical growth for nine months, the baby died.

The devastation of delivering an ill-formed and apparently severely retarded infant was more than the parents could bear. Their agony, particularly that of the mother, turned to hostility. As is often the case, that hostility was directed toward the one who had delivered the baby. Dr. Dorrough had conscientiously provided her with his usual high-quality care, but he was charged with malicious, intentional, "wanton" negligence in a malpractice suit (later changed to "wrongful death"). Both compensatory and punitive damages sufficient to prevent the defendant "from inflicting such willful and wanton acts in the future" were demanded.

Dr. Dorrough was completely crushed by the allegations in the malpractice suit, among which were that the plaintiff should have been met by Dr. Dorrough at the hospital upon her arrival; she should have remained connected to the fetal monitor without the usual preparation procedures; and no enema should have been given (even though examination revealed the cervix to be completely undilated). It was further alleged that a "crash" general anesthetic, rather than a spinal, should have been performed within fifteen minutes.

Dr. Dorrough carried only the usual one million dollar malpractice insurance policy. Alabama law provides that, if the amount of punitive damages awarded in a "wrongful death" suit exceeds the defendant's insurance coverage, a distinct possibility in today's climate, the plaintiff can take all of the defendant's assets, including house, automobile, savings, and pension fund and then attach *all future earnings* until the awarded claim is paid. Filing for bankruptcy by the defendant to protect future earnings is not allowable. Although the suggested amount of the suit was $25 million, Dr. Dorrough's attorney predicted that, if the jury ruled in favor of the plaintiff, the award would be in the neighborhood of $5 million, making complete financial ruin for him a distinct possibility.

Dr. Dorrough, a solo practitioner, had to spend an inordinate amount of time away from his practice, attending over sixty depositions all around the country. Accustomed to being treated with dignity and respect, he was totally unprepared for the viciousness of the "hired guns" he encountered. He felt that they had been misled by the plaintiffs' distortions of what had actually happened and were, therefore, out to get him.

The trial itself was also difficult, dividing the community in many respects. Baptist Medical Center, where the baby was delivered, was named in the lawsuit. The baby's great-uncle was Chairman of the Board of Directors there and was a personal friend of Dr. Dorrough, who also served on that Board. The two families were well known in town and had many friends in common. Both were active members of the Baptist denomination, which created a situation in which many church members felt caught in the middle. There were many prayers offered during the trial and pre-trial periods, but all were not praying for the same thing.

During the trial, Mrs. Dorrough had arranged for friends of hers to pray each day as they sat in the courtroom. Each morning they would decide ahead of time which scripture they would use and then silently pray the same thing as the day progressed. One day they were all praying that the plaintiffs' lawyers would "ensnare themselves with their own deceit." At the end of that particular day the plaintiffs decided to present evidence from the deposition of a witness who was not going to testify in person at the trial. The way that is done in court is for one of the plaintiffs' attorneys to sit on the witness stand in place of the absent witness and read the responses recorded in the deposition, while the other plaintiffs' attorney asks selected questions from the deposition. The plaintiffs' attorneys had carefully marked all of the questions they planned to read, but they had brought only one copy of the deposition to the trial that day. Unable to locate another copy, the attorney who was to ask the questions borrowed a copy from Dr. Dorrough's attorney which had also been carefully marked — but with the questions most advantageous for the defense. Amazingly, the plantiffs' attorney did not catch on until after he had unwittingly brought out all of the points the defense had wanted to make. There was no doubt in the minds of those who were praying, that there had been some Divine intervention in court that day.

After a two-week trial, it took the jury only forty-five minutes to rule in Dr. Dorrough's favor; but the experience had been agonizing for him. It left a bitter taste at the end of an otherwise rewarding career. He knew that he had provided the patient with excellent care and could not have possibly altered the outcome, yet he was charged with willful and wanton malpractice. After a lifetime of hearing people praise him for his kindness, love, and devotion, he had to listen to a barrage of charges that he was a negligent physician.

The allegations of the plaintiffs were untrue, but even if *everything* they said had been true, the *most* Dr. Dorrough could have been guilty of was a conscientious error in judgment. Who among us, regardless of our profession, does not make judgmental errors regularly? Who among us is perfect?

There are those in society who spend much of their time thinking of ways that they can get ahead by cheating others. When they are caught, the most we do to them is make them pay a fine or spend a period of time in jail before allowing them to continue their lives where they left off. There is something terribly, terribly wrong with a system which treats criminals that way but takes a dedicated man who has devoted his whole life to serving others and places him in jeopardy of losing *everything* he has — past and even future earnings — when his worst offense is said to be that he made a human error.

Dr. Dorrough is now retired. Dr. Cheek contemplates giving up caring for high risk babies. Dr. Nabors contemplates giving up medicine altogether. They are representative of what is going on all over the country. God help us.

Chapter 3

Nothing can be lasting when
reason does not rule.
—Quintus Curtius Rufus

The medical malpractice litigation crisis in this country is real. Its extent is not generally appreciated by the public, but it is beginning to have a devastating effect on the ability of many Americans to obtain high quality care at any price. Physicians everywhere, in record numbers, are leaving their practices or limiting their services. One fourth of doctors in Florida have stopped delivering babies. Twenty-four percent of orthopedists and *seventy* percent of obstetricians in Massachusetts are refusing to take new patients.

Cullman County recently became the twenty-fourth county in Alabama to lose its obstetrical services when a jury returned a $2.5 million verdict against the physicians for transferring a high risk mother to Birmingham to deliver her premature infant. The jury bought the plaintiff's argument that the delay, not the prematurity, caused the baby's injuries. The obstetricians, damned if they deliver high risk babies and damned if they don't decided to hang it up.

Astronomical judgments against physicians are skyrocketing. Juries in Mobile, Alabama, awarded $22.5 million in a four week period in three separate malpractice suits against physicians. A New York jury recently set a record by awarding $65 million, including $58 million in punitive damages, to a woman who had a delay in diagnosis of her intestinal obstruction.

Barry Furrow, law professor at the University of Detroit, insists that a small percentage of physicians are responsible for most of the lawsuits. He is joined by none other than Ralph Nader, who claims that "bad apples" among physicians have caused the dramatic increases in malpractice premiums. These opinions fly in the face of irrefutable facts to the contrary. Thirty percent of physicians who graduated from medical schools in the United States and practice in New York City have been sued for malpractice. Sixty percent of obstetricians in the United States have been sued. Surely most doctors are not incompetent.

Studies conducted by the Medical Liability Mutual Insurance Company and the National Association of Insurance Commissioners have clearly shown that the major factor influencing the frequency of litigation is not the competency of the doctor but the complexity of the illness. The frequency of imperfect results increases with the complexity of the illness. Paradoxically, according to the study, surgeons with the most training, who performed the most complex operations, were the ones most frequently sued. Malpractice suits and "bad apples" are not synonymous.

Although malpractice surely exists among physicians, as it does among lawyers, engineers, architects, psychologists, and any other profession imaginable, it is naive to attribute the current litigation problem to "a few bad apples." There is no more malpractice in medicine than there is in any other field. The problem is that we live in a society that has gone suit-crazy.

Gov. George Wallace, his ear ever to the ground, perceived the rumblings around him in the medical profession and in society as a whole. A lawyer and a former judge himself, he has a keen understanding of what is going on. He devoted a portion of his address to the legislature on the opening day of the 1986 session to the liability crisis.

> Everybody is suing everybody else and the courts are jammed with all kinds of lawsuits . . . , many of them frivolous. Nobody wants victims to be unprotected, but judges and juries are handing out unbelievable judgments against people who did not create the problem in the first place, but who are thought to be financially able to pay large judgments.
>
> When doctors see every patient as a potential lawsuit, and other professionals see every service or job as a potential malpractice hazard, it's time for something to be done. Too many qualified professionals are leaving their field of expertise because they cannot obtain malpractice insurance, or it's so high they can't afford it.
>
> And it's not just doctors and midwives who are affected. We're also talking about engineers, accountants, educators, retail businesses, industries, and manufacturers of products.
>
> I'll tell you what's happening: trial lawyers are getting fat,

and everybody else is paying through the nose. In fact, one study in 1984 showed that in one non-medical field, lawyer's fees consumed an astonishing sixty-three percent of court damage awards. And in the medical area, the number of malpractice cases in Alabama has doubled since 1980, and the average jury award has jumped from $57,000 to $1.9 million in the last four years.

This is not just a medical problem. It's not just a business problem. It's everybody's problem because it's the people who have to pay for it in the long run. I say it's time we take action to reduce the amounts of these judgments that will allow our people to continue to receive important services.

Governor Wallace was exactly right. It is not just a medical malpractice problem, but one which is ubiquitous in our society. A sickness has pervaded our country in recent years — the delusion that nothing ever goes wrong by chance. Where there is misfortune, there must be someone to blame, and the villain must make restitution. Deplorably, the one to whom the blame is often assigned is not determined by his degree of culpability, but by the depths of his pockets.

A man in California was standing in a phone booth beside the road when a drunken driver lost control of her car and slammed into the phone booth, injuring the occupant. The California Supreme Court ruled it perfectly acceptable to assign the liability to the companies who designed and installed the booth rather than the drunken driver. A man in New York City attempted to commit suicide by jumping in front of a subway train, then sued the city because the driver did not stop soon enough to avoid hitting him. He was awarded $650,000 in an out-of-court settlement. Newspapers and magazines are replete with similar stories, where the blame has been assigned, not to the negligent or foolish individual, but to the individual or the entity with the most money. Some of these decisions that are being made by a small minority of the population are having devastating consequences on society members as a whole.

Cities everywhere are being forced to close swimming pools and parks because they can no longer afford liability protection. Resort and recreation areas are becoming more expensive as the owners pass on the cost of liability insurance to the consumer. Day care centers are closing. Pharmaceutical companies are questioning the wisdom of continuing to offer products essential to our health, because virtually every medication has some inherent risk. Unless something is changed, we may again face the epidemics of the past, because our children will no longer be able to get vaccinations against diphtheria, whooping cough, and tetanus. A vial of this vaccine (DPT) once sold for only pennies. That price increased to $5.43 in 1981 and to $65.00 in 1985. The increases were brought about, largely, by exorbitant jury awards to children who have had rare reactions to the vaccine. Soon the price is to increase to $171 a vial and, ultimately, it may not be available at any price.

Polio, which killed or crippled tens of thousands each year a few decades ago, was drastically curtailed to only a few thousand cases a year by the development of the Salk vaccine. That vaccine, made from dead polio viruses, was not as effective in preventing polio as the Sabin vaccine, later made from alive but weakened polio viruses. Although the live vaccine could rarely cause polio — about one case out of two million doses — it afforded far greater protection for the vast majority of Americans, and became the vaccine of preference according to official U. S. policy. In 1984, a Kansas City jury awarded $10 million, including $8 million in punitive damages, to a man who had contracted polio from the vaccine which was given to his infant daughter. The jury thought it "outrageous" to sell the Sabin vaccine, when the Salk vaccine is safer. There are more than 150 lawsuits, totaling more than $2 billion, pending against the vaccine nationally. A handful of misinformed jurors, deceived by avaricious attorneys, are making judgments which are imposing severe penalties on all of society.

When will it end? Will the greed of a few destroy the very foundation of our society? I think not. Change will inevitably come. It will not come from lawyers. It will not come from doctors. It will not come from judges. It will not come from juries. It will come from the multitude of people who make up the fabric of our society. There will come a time when enough people will realize that a few are beginning to interfere with the inalienable rights of all, depriving them of access to goods and services required for their health and happiness. The time will come when enough people finally realize that it is *they* who bear the cost of the obscene bonanzas awarded to a few. The time will come when enough people look around them and realize that they cannot find a physician to care for them in their time of greatest need, or deliver their babies, or immunize their children. And when they do — when enough people come to those realizations — from the beaches of Key West to the desolate wilderness beside the Yukon — from the bustling streets of Manhattan to the quiet hamlets on the prairie — the *people* will cry out in that loud, resounding, collective voice that makes America great, "Enough! Enough! We have had quite enough!" Then, and only then will change come, and reason, sanity, and justice finally prevail.

Chapter 4

January, 1981-April, 1983

Diseases, desperate grown,
by desperate appliance are
relieved, or not at all.
—Shakespeare

The case of Kathy Roberts (a pseudonym) is tragic. Fate, Providence, or whatever force there is in this universe that capriciously visits misfortune upon individuals, had been unkind to her. At the age of twenty-six, soon after the birth of her second child, she began having bouts of severe abdominal pain. She was referred to a gastroenterologist, a specialist in intestinal disorders, who performed a proctoscopic exam which failed to reveal a cause for her symptoms. The severe pain persisted, leading her gynecologist to undertake an exploratory operation in January, 1981. Much to his surprise he found a relatively rare problem for someone so young. A large cancer had grown undetected and eaten a hole all the way through the colon wall, spilling bowel contents and pus into her pelvis, forming a large abscess. Her gynecologist, trained to handle surgical problems involving the uterus, ovaries, and tubes, realized he had encountered a complex problem originating in her colon, an area outside the realm of his expertise. He summoned my partner, Dr. John Cameron, to the operating room to take over the care of this seriously ill patient as she lay anesthetized on the operating table.

In the eyes of many, Dr. Cameron was one of the very finest surgeons in all of Alabama. For over a quarter of a century, patients from all over southeastern Alabama had been referred to him for surgical care. His excellent training, his skill in the operating room, and his dedication to remaining current in his knowledge were unsurpassed by any surgeon in the area. There had been countless times since his arrival in Montgomery in 1949, fresh out of his residency training at the Mayo Clinic, that he had been called into the operating room to take over a case when the operating surgeon had unexpectedly encountered a situation that he could not handle. John Cameron thrived on challenges. He loved to work on the sickest patients who had the most complex problems and most desperately needed skillful care in order to survive. And he did it well. In his thirty-one years of practice he had never had a lawsuit filed against him.

After scrubbing and entering the operating room, Dr. Cameron carefully evaluated the large tumor mass in Kathy's colon, along with the severe inflammation and infection it had caused. He then skillfully proceeded to remove the cancerous segment of colon, drain the pus from the abscess, and construct a colostomy so that her intestines would move into a bag on her abdomen. It was a major, life-threatening illness that she had, but her recovery was remarkable. She was up and around in no time, and went home a week after the operation.

When cancer is confined to the colon, as it was in President Reagan, the chance of removing it all with an operation is greater than fifty percent. However, when it has eaten all the way through the colon wall and spilled into the pelvic region, the chance that it will recur is overwhelming. Well aware of this fact, Dr. Cameron followed Kathy closely in office examinations during the ensuing weeks. As feared, less than three months later he detected a mass of cancer that had rapidly grown and was then distinguishable from the surrounding scar tissue. A needle biopsy (a test in which a small piece of tissue is taken with a needle for microscopic examination) confirmed his suspicions that she had a recurrent cancer.

Her outlook at that point was dismal indeed. There was still a small possibility that the cancer could be removed with another operation, but the procedure required would be formidable. The infection and previous operation had left her pelvis filled with scar tissue, distorting the anatomy in the region into a barely recognizable conglomerate. In order to attempt to get around all of the cancer, it would be necessary to perform an operation called a pelvic exenteration, in which her uterus, her fallopian tubes, her ovaries, part of her rectum, part of her vagina, and perhaps even part of her bladder, would be removed. This surgical procedure is so extensive that there would be a ten to fifteen percent chance that she would not survive it and would never leave the hospital alive. If she did survive the procedure, the chance that a few undetectable cancer cells would be left behind to grow and take her life over the next three to four years was eighty-five to ninety percent. So even with this radical operation she had, at best, one chance in ten of being cured. But it was her only chance. Without the operation, she would certainly succumb to the cancer within a few years.

Dr. Cameron carefully explained to Kathy and her husband what they were up against, that the operation was her only hope for cure but the results might be devastating. He made it clear to them that the operation had substantial risks and that there would likely be substantial changes in her life style as a result of it. Faced with no viable options, they consented to proceed. On April 23, 1981, Dr. Cameron embarked on an attempt to save her life with a radical operation.

Dr. Cameron always hated to give up on a difficult cancer operation when he knew that he alone stood between the patient and death. Painstakingly and meticulously he would continue the dissection as long as there was a glimmer of hope that he could get the cancer out. Years ago he and his partner, Dr. Jack Till, were attempting to remove a stomach cancer which had grown into adjacent organs. Someone came to the door of the operating room to inquire what they were doing. Dr. Till turned and replied, "It's inoperable, but John's going to take it out anyway." I had that same feeling as I was helping him with Kathy's operation. The mass of scar tissue had tightly bound down all of the pelvic structures, including the ureters, which are tubes that carry urine from the kidneys to the bladder. I felt certain that I could not have removed the cancer, and I did not believe he could.

But he did. It has been over five years since that operation, and Kathy Roberts does not have a trace of cancer in her body. As far as anyone can tell, she is one of the fortunate few to be cured of recurrent colon cancer. But that cure did not come without a substantial price.

A cardinal principle of cancer surgery is that one must remove a wide margin of normal tissue around the cancer in order to be sure that the cancer is totally encompassed. Unfortunately, when one does this radical, complex surgery, there is a significant risk of developing major complications. When the tissues are grossly distorted by scarring from previous infection and surgery, injury to surrounding structures is often unavoidable. In removing Kathy's cancer Dr. Cameron cut her right ureter, immediately recognized it and appropriately repaired it. She suffered no permanent disability as a result of the cut ureter and today has two normally functioning kidneys and ureters.

Unfortunately, totally unrelated to the severed ureter, Kathy developed some severe, unavoidable complications of surgery and nearly died. We struggled long and hard to keep her alive, and we succeeded. When all was said and done, she was left with an amputated left leg and a stroke which paralyzed the right side of her body. It was tragic, and we grieved with her. She was in the hospital for almost two months before going home to continue rehabilitation. She learned to walk with an artificial leg and now barely limps. Her paralysis gradually cleared, leaving her with no perceptible weakness or disability. We rejoiced as the months passed without evidence of recurrent cancer, and it became more apparent that she was to be one of the fortunate few who are cured by the operation.

Two years after the operation (one day before the statute of limitations expired) my partners and I were served with a summons which I read in disbelief. Kathy Roberts was suing us for malpractice. The suit alleged that we were negligent in inadvertently severing her ureter while performing the posterior pelvic exenteration, and that we failed to order proper and adequate follow-up care and supervision. Kathy was alleged to have suffered permanent injuries as a "proximate result" of these acts.

The summons marked the beginning of a pilgrimage I was to take through the inner working of our legal system — a pilgrimage that would leave me disillusioned and discouraged. I gradually came to see that in our "adversarial" system neither side is interested in an objective, unbiased appraisal of the events in question. Both sides just want to win. It is a system which regularly turns patients against their doctors, and their doctors, in turn, against them. It is a system which only sporadically rewards the ones who need it the most — the poor, unfortunate patients. It is a system which rewards attorneys handsomely. For a plaintiff's attorney it is a lottery. He will lose most of the time, but he only has to win occasionally to become wealthy. The defense attorney is paid the same, win or lose. Naturally, the more cases he wins, the more he will be asked to defend. If the defense attorney is good and wins most of his cases, the system rewards him handsomely. I ultimately came to the inescapable conclusion that our legal system as currently structured benefits primarily attorneys at a tremendous cost to society. It is no small wonder that the strongest defenders of the system are attorneys. I joined the growing host of critics who believe that medical malpractice lawsuits have no place in the jury system — and never did.

Chapter 5

The right to a trial by jury has become such a revered part of our system of jurisprudence that to suggest a variance from that tradition would be considered to be, at least, unpatriotic and, more likely, heretical. However, our "common law" tradition, in existence since the Battle of Hastings in A.D. 1066, is not nearly as revered and respected around the world as the much older and more widespread "civil law" tradition, which dates its origin to 450 B. C. In fact, many have referred to our system as being "feudal, barbaric and uncouth."[1] The aspect of our tradition which is particularly revered in this country, the right to a trial by jury, is essentially non-existent in other traditions, and much less prominent in common law countries other than the United States.

Our jury system really originated during the reign of Henry II, who ruled England from 1154 until 1189. The system was implemented in order to give landowners an alternative to settling disputes by a duel, a progressive move that few today would fault. The original jurors were all knights and were required to independently familiarize themselves with the facts involved in the disputes. Gradually, over the next two hundred years, the requirement that jurors be knights was eased, and the most highly respected members of a community were also allowed to serve. During that same period of time, jurors ceased to familiarize themselves with the facts of a case ahead of time, but became impartial judges of the facts presented to them at trials. This jury system was the one our forefathers were familiar with when they came to the new world.

One of the reasons for the separation of the colonies from England as stated in the Declaration of Independence was "For depriving us, in many cases, of the benefits of Trial by Jury." The United States Constitution guaranteed that "the trial of all crimes . . . shall be by jury. . . ." There was no guarantee of a jury trial in civil cases, a fact that disturbed many of the founding fathers, among whom were Thomas Jefferson and Alexander Hamilton. Accordingly, when the Constitution was amended with the Bill of Rights, the seventh amendment guaranteed that "in suits at common law, where the value in controversy shall exceed twenty dollars, the right of trial by jury shall be preserved. . . ."

Without question, the intent of the seventh amendment

was to assure an individual the right to be tried by an impartial panel of peers who could understand and relate to his problems. In many situations it does just that. However, in the area of medical malpractice, that very same amendment, in fact, deprives physicians of the opportunity to be tried by a group of their peers — people who can understand and accurately judge the complexities of the issues involved.

Two hundred years ago medical malpractice was just not in the minds of our founding fathers. Negligence of any kind was not a major issue of the day — nor of the next three quarters of a century. Eventually, however, the changes wrought by the Industrial Revolution had a substantial impact on the legal climate in this country. The development and widespread use of the locomotive ushered in the beginnings of our society's preoccupation with civil litigation for negligence. The "Iron Horse" was a two-edged sword. It provided rapid transportation of people and materials across the countryside, but it also exacted its toll on the lives and limbs of those people and animals who encountered it.

In the mid-portion of the nineteenth century, contingency legal fees were not generally accepted as being ethical. However, over the next few decades, their use in this country became almost universal; and civil litigation mushroomed. In a contingency system, an attorney takes a plaintiff's case with an agreement to be paid a percentage of the awarded proceeds, if any. The percentage varies but is usually one-third to one-half of the award, and the attorneys share is usually taken from the *total* amount, the expenses of the trial being deducted from the plaintiff's share. The United States is one of the few remaining nations in which contingency fees are considered ethical, and the only country in the world in which unregulated contingency fees exist.

Not a single treatise on the subject of torts (civil wrongs,

including negligence) was published in the United States
prior to 1850. By the turn of the century the literature
was replete with such references. The combination of the
contingency fee system providing an incentive for attorneys
to file negligence suits, and the ability of the attorneys to
manipulate sympathetic jurors, was largely responsible for
this evolution in our country.

England, in the twentieth century, joined most of the rest
of the world and removed civil litigation from the jury
system. In 1933, the general right to a civil jury was abol-
ished, except in cases of fraud.

Distinguished voices have been raised in this century ad-
vising that we in the United States abandon our obsession
with maintaining the status quo. An article appeared in the
American Bar Association Journal in 1924 which was extremely critical of our jury system. Among other things
the author wrote:

> Too long has the effete and sterile jury system been per-
> mitted to tug at the throat of the nation's judiciary as it
> sinks under the smothering deluge of the obloquy of those
> it was designed to serve. Too long has ignorance been per-
> mitted to sit ensconced in the places of judicial administra-
> tion where knowledge is so sorely needed. Too long has the
> lament of the Shakespearean character been echoed, 'Justice
> has fled to brutish beasts and men have lost their reason.'[2]

Jerome Frank, a leading critic of the jury system, wrote:

> I submit that the jury is the worst possible enemy of that
> ideal of the 'supremacy of law.' For jury-made law is par
> excellence, capricious and arbitrary, yielding to the maxi-
> mum in way of lack of uniformity, and of unknowability.'[3]

More recently, Leon Sarky wrote:

> Related to present day American life, civil jury trials represent the horse and buggy segment of American administration of justice, reflecting a judicial provincialism and a mid-Victorian drag on our judicial process, which calls for realistic treatment by way of reform.[4]

The Dean of the Harvard Law School, in his 1963 annual report, wrote:

> Why should anyone think that 12 persons brought in from the street, selected in various ways for their lack of general ability, should have any special capacity for deciding controversies between persons?[5]

The twelve persons do not have any special capacity for resolving controversies. In fact, the means of selecting jurors often insures that they will be even less capable than the ordinary population of understanding the issues involved.

So why do we maintain such a system? Why do we cling to an archaic method of handling modern problems when that method serves our needs so poorly? Because that system is advantageous to the multitude of lawyers in this country, and lawyers make the laws. The rest of us blindly accept the system as it is. We accept it in part because we are complacent, but mostly because we are uninformed.

Thus it was that Dr. Cameron and I had to prepare ourselves for an encounter with a jury — not a jury of our peers, but a jury of people who, try as they may, were simply not equipped to sort out conflicting testimony and figure out where the truth lay. We had to adapt ourselves to a system which was alien to the way we were accustomed to thinking and behaving. I knew very little about that system when I first started preparing for our trial.

Chapter 6

April 21, 1983

Where are the evidence that do
accuse me?
—Shakespeare

t had been almost two years since Kathy's hospitalization when we received the summons, and
the details of her illness were fuzzy in my mind.
What care in the postoperative period could they
possibly be referring to as substandard? To my knowledge
she had received excellent care but had sustained her disabilities as an unavoidable result of her cancer and the radical

nature of the treatment which was necessary to cure her.

After obtaining a copy of the hospital record, I began to review it and discovered that I had been primarily responsible for her care while Dr. Cameron was on vacation during the first week after the operation. I immediately focused on that first week to see if, in retrospect, I could identify any problem areas. On the first postoperative day she had a temperature of 101, certainly well within the range that one would expect after such an extensive operation. On the second day her temperature was not higher than 100.8. I noticed that I had appropriately stopped her antibiotics at that time, and her low-grade fever had continued to decrease daily until it was completely gone by the seventh day. A large amount of urine had been leaking from the site where the ureter was repaired, but it was being carried to the outside of her body by the drains Dr. Cameron had left for that purpose. No problem there. There would have been nothing to do at that point but wait for the drainage to gradually stop. A review of the nurses' notes revealed that, in general, Kathy had been doing quite well that week, walking in the hall, smoking, watching television, visiting with her friends, having a friend wash her hair, etc. By the end of the week it looked as if she was well on her way to another relatively uneventful recovery as she had had in January. I noted that Dr. Ingalls, another partner in the practice, was on call the next weekend, then Dr. Cameron returned and once again assumed primary care. I was satisfied that, even in retrospect, the care which I had delivered was as near to perfect as possible, and the alleged "substandard care" must have related to some other period of her two-month hospital stay. I assumed that I was being named in the suit because plaintiffs' attorneys always seem to name all the members of the group when they sue one member. They had even named our youngest associate, Duncan McRae, even though, at the time Kathy was in the hospital, he was still a resident at the University of Virginia and had not even joined our group.

The remainder of the chart was complex, but I knew I needed to review it as well to see if I could discern any basis for the suit. Kathy had continued to do well for about five more days. Then, on the thirteenth postoperative day, she developed a fever of 101.4, the first time her temperature had been above 101 during her hospitalization.

A urine culture (a test for the presence or absence of bacteria in the urine) had shown evidence of a minor infection. All patients after a pelvic exenteration, whether a ureter is cut or not, have difficulty voiding for a period of time and require a catheter to empty the bladder. Due to bacterial contamination along the catheter, many of them develop urinary tract infections, and Kathy was no exception.

Kathy also developed thrombophlebitis, a combination of clotting and inflammation within the veins, which is a well-recognized, unavoidable complication of surgery, particularly major pelvic surgery. The risk of developing it is increased in patients with cancer and obesity. Kathy's 180 pound weight at the time of her operation, coupled with the other factors, placed her at great risk. On the very first day that she experienced any pain or swelling in her leg, a special x-ray called a venogram was done which confirmed the presence of thrombophlebitis in her left leg, and she was promptly started on an anticoagulant, or blood thinner, *Heparin*.

It was not clear to me, even in retrospect, whether the low grade fever she had was caused by the urinary tract infection, or whether it was an early manifestation of the thrombophlebitis. It didn't really matter. Both conditions had been recognized and managed appropriately. I was having a difficult time thus far finding anything that remotely resembled negligence in her care.

As I continued to thumb through the chart I saw Kathy's phlebitis improved on the *Heparin* therapy, and she seemed to be recovering satisfactorily until three weeks after the operation when she suddenly became desperately ill. Her blood pressure dropped and she went into shock, developing a rapid, weak pulse. The dark blue color of her lips and nail beds indicated that she was perilously close to death. She was immediately transferred to the Intensive Care Unit and placed on a respirator. Dr. Cameron's speculation at that time, reflected in the progress notes, was that a blood clot had broken loose from the area of thrombophlebitis and gone to her lung (a so-called pulmonary embolus) or that she could have possibly developed sepsis (an infection which has invaded the bloodstream). He also noted that he was wondering if there could be a possible relationship between *Heparin* and the precipitous change in Kathy's condition. Because of the grave nature of her illness, there was no time to lose in initiating the appropriate therapy. She was immediately started on high doses of antibiotics to treat any possible sepsis. A pulmonary specialist was called in for consultation, and because the platelet count in her blood, one of the factors involved in blood clotting, was inexplicably low, a hematologist was also consulted. It soon became apparent that, in addition to whatever caused her shock, she had also developed a stroke, so a neurologist was brought in. The chart reflected that all of these doctors had worked diligently to save the life of this dying girl.

Because of the likelihood that blood clots were breaking loose from the veins in her legs or pelvis and going to her lungs, clots that could conceivably be infected, a decision was made to operate and tie off the inferior vena cava, the major vein through which blood returns from the lower part of the body to the heart and lungs. This would prevent even small additional clots from reaching the lungs. Dr. Cameron and Dr. Ingalls performed the procedure and, in the process, specifically looked for any evidence of infection in her pelvis, finding none. The leakage of urine from the repaired ureter had almost stopped by that time, but as an added safety measure, the urologist who had supervised the repair of the severed ureter inserted a tube into the kidney (a procedure called a nephrostomy) to drain urine to the outside, bypassing the injured ureter until it had completely healed. Despite the fact that no infection had been found, therapy with antibiotics was continued for a period of time just to be certain that there was no potentially lethal condition being left untreated. Kathy gradually improved and ultimately survived this catastrophic illness. During her hospitalization, she began to develop a decreased blood supply to her left foot, a problem which occasionally develops when the swelling from thrombophlebitis is severe. An operation called a fasciotomy was performed in an attempt to release the pressure on the arteries and improve the blood supply to her foot, but the surgery was to no avail. She eventually developed gangrene in her foot and had to have her leg amputated below the knee.

Still, I could find nothing in the record that would suggest substandard care. My only area of concern was that I could not explain why she had a stroke. It just didn't fit. The blood clots from her leg could not have traveled to her brain. They would have been filtered by her lungs. Infection, even if she had it, would not have caused a stroke. I was still as baffled by the stroke as we all had been when she was in the hospital, but I was confident it wasn't caused by negligence.

After completing my review of the records I could find no evidence of substandard care by any of the physicians who had treated her. Since I had not even been involved in her care during the period of time when she was critically ill, I was certain that the charges of negligence did not refer to the care I had provided for her. At least for the time being, I put the case in the back of my mind and tried not to dwell on it.

Chapter 7

Fall, 1983

Happy the man who has been able
to understand the causes of things.
—Vergil

I thought of the lawsuit very little during the next few months, but it was obviously weighing heavily on Dr. Cameron's mind. I worried about him. Frequently, when I would walk past his office door, I would see him sitting at his desk, staring blankly out the window. I knew, without asking, what he was thinking about. He spent countless hours poring over Kathy's chart, thinking about all aspects of the case, critically evaluating the care he had given, and reviewing voluminous books and articles in the medical literature. I began to feel guilty that I wasn't spending more of my time helping him prepare.

One day Dr. Cameron walked into my office beaming with excitement. In his hand was a recent surgical journal which contained an article that had caught his attention. The article described several patients just like Kathy who had unexpectedly developed gangrene of the extremities, or strokes, or both. The common denominator in all of the patients was that they had a rare allergic reaction to *Heparin*, the blood thinner that Kathy had been receiving for her phlebitis when she became desperately ill. Dr. Cameron thought that this allergic reaction to *Heparin* might have caused clotting throughout Kathy's body and had caused her stroke and contributed to the need for her leg amputation.

I went back through the chart, checking out his new theory, and found that everything fit perfectly. The catastrophic day on which she almost died was seven days after the *Heparin* was started — the same interval as the other patients described in the article. The reaction takes place after the patient has had time to develop antibodies to the *Heparin*. The antibodies circulate in the blood stream along with small cells called platelets (or thrombocytes) which are important in the formation of blood clots. Unfortunately, the antibodies occasionally interact with the platelets in a manner that causes them to stick together and form clots in the small vessels throughout the body.

The number of platelets present in the blood can be measured by a relatively simple blood test. Normally the platelet count is at least 160,000 cells per cubic millimeter of blood. When there is an allergic reaction to *Heparin*, the platelet count in the blood drops precipitously as the platelets are used up by the clotting that is occurring within the blood vessels. Kathy's platelet count on her sickest day was 18,000, which is extremely low. Until now we had not completely understood why. Dr. Cameron had noted in the progress notes at the time that *Heparin* possibly could have been responsible for the low platelets, and he had consulted a hematologist that same day. Little was known at that time about the relationship of *Heparin* to low platelets and its significance was not generally appreciated. The hematologist did not believe at the time that Kathy's severe illness was being caused by the drug. She had continued to receive full doses of *Heparin* for two days after the stroke occurred, and she had remained critically ill. It was at that time that she was operated upon again to tie off her vena cava and to look for sepsis. No sepsis was found, which was surprising then, but completely understandable now. Her *Heparin* dosage was decreased markedly after the operation and it was stopped completely five days later — a serendipitous event which probably contributed to her continued improvement and ultimate survival.

At long last we understood the cause of Kathy's stroke. Her allergic reaction to *Heparin* had caused thrombosis (clotting) of the arteries in the left side of the brain. As a result of the clotted blood vessels, the brain cells did not receive enough oxygen. The inevitable result of this oxygen deprivation was a stroke. Dr. Cameron's discovery also explained why her phlebitis progressed to the point of gangrene. She obviously had developed clots in the small vessels of her left foot as well, depriving the foot of blood flow and oxygen. It also explained her acute deterioration three weeks after the operation. She had almost surely been developing clots in the small vessels of her lungs at the same time. Everything fit.

My first impulse was to show Kathy and her lawyer what

had been published in the medical literature since she had
been hospitalized, and explain to them that we now understood what had happened. She had not had sepsis at all, and
certainly none of her subsequent medical problems was related to the cut ureter. I later discovered I was thinking like
most physicians do in similar circumstances: if only I can explain the complex medical details to the plaintiff's attorney,
he will understand the truth, be satisfied, and drop the case.
The fallacy in this reasoning is that plaintiffs' attorneys are
not necessarily concerned with the truth. Their obligation is
not to insure justice but to advocate their client's claims to
the best of their ability. Likewise, defendants' attorneys are
not burdened primarily with a compelling desire to insure justice. They, too, just want to win. Ours is an adversarial system in which neither side seeks what is right and fair. Both
present their cases in the best possible light, while others are
the "seekers of truth." Unfortunately, the "seekers of
truth," the jurors, are not equipped to evaluate the complex
issues involved in a medical malpractice trial. The physician,
therefore, has no choice but to play the lawyers' game. Gradually, I learned from our attorneys that I was not going to
be able to present our side of the case with unbridled candor.
I was to completely reorient my thinking in order to survive
this lawsuit. After years of objectively analyzing data, judging it critically, and presenting it in an unbiased manner, I
was going to have to begin thinking like a lawyer — how the
truth can be presented at the best possible time, in the best
possible manner, in order to insure an ultimate judgment in
our favor.

I suppose there is a remote possibility that the plaintiff's
attorney would have dropped the suit had we explained what
we knew about *Heparin* as soon as we knew it. There is also
a remote possibility the Pope may become a Baptist, but it

would be unwise to count on it. The odds seemed overwhelming that we would only allow the plaintiff to better prepare for the trial by divulging this information about *Heparin*.

In countries whose legal systems stem from a civil rather than a common law tradition, this problem does not arise. There is no such thing as a "trial" where everyone gathers at a specific time to lay their entire case on the line. Rather, there is a series of meetings between the attorneys and judges in which evidence is introduced and testimony given. There is little, if any, advantage to the element of surprise, since the opposing attorney has ample time to research and attempt to refute any points introduced. There is no need to try to keep the opposing attorney from "discovering" everything that will be introduced at a trial.

There is something terribly wrong with a system that encourages holding an ace to the bitter end of a long and costly ordeal — an ace that, if shown early enough, might even cause the opponent to fold.

Chapter 8

July, 1984

*When all is done, the help of
good counsel is that which
setteth business straight again.*
—Francis Bacon

*B*y the mid-1970s our society was rapidly becoming more litigious and the number of lawsuits being filed was increasing exponentially. The explosion of medical malpractice litigation which had rocked California and New York was spreading all over the country. Alabama was no exception. Insurance companies were finding it increasingly difficult to predict future losses. They were fearful of losing huge sums of money if juries in Alabama followed the national trend of awarding multi-million dollar settlements. Consequently, St. Paul Fire and Marine Insurance Company, a major malpractice underwriter, stopped writing new policies for physicians. Aetna Life Insurance Company and Employers Insurance of Wausau pulled out altogether, not even renewing existing coverage and leaving doctors with nowhere to turn. A crisis ensued. With no viable alternatives, a large number of doctors in Alabama joined together and formed their own professional liability insurance company, The Mutual Assurance Society of Alabama. Mutual Assurance wanted to serve notice to plaintiffs' attorneys in Alabama that the trend prevalent in other parts of the country would not be followed. They did not intend to settle cases simply to avoid the expense of a long battle and the potential risk of losing a huge jury award. They intended to vigorously fight to the end in every case that was without merit. Plaintiffs' attorneys could not file frivolous cases with the expectation of having them settled out of court for substantial sums of money.

In order to prepare for the hard battles ahead, Mutual Assurance wanted to employ attorneys with the most experience in trying medical malpractice cases. It was ironic that they turned to Charlie Stakely, a young Montgomery attorney who was a partner in his father's law firm, Rushton, Stakely, Johnston and Garrett. Stakely's total experience with medical malpractice trials consisted of a case in the mid-sixties in which he defended Montgomery Baptist Hospital, and a case a few years later in which he defended several physicians. He won both cases and, by virtue of those two trials, established himself as the most experienced malpractice defense attorney around. There had just not been much medical malpractice litigation, or civil litigation of any kind for that matter, prior to that time. In Montgomery County in 1975 there were three dockets a year at the courthouse for civil cases, each docket lasting three weeks. All of the civil cases in a year were tried in a nine-week period. A decade later civil cases are now tried fifty-two weeks a year.

After establishing an alliance with Mutual Assurance, Charlie Stakely's experience with malpractice mushroomed. Over the next few years he established a reputation in Alabama (and even around the country) as a premier malpractice defense attorney. Within a few years his case load was more than he could handle alone, and he tapped a young associate, Tommy Keene, to work with him in the area of malpractice defense. Keene had joined the firm after graduating from the University of Alabama School of Law in 1974 and had become a full partner two and one-half years later, the fastest anyone had accomplished that feat in the ninety-year history of the firm. Within a few years both Stakely and Keene were devoting almost all of their professional time to malpractice defense litigation.

Our case was assigned to Keene, and he immediately felt as much pressure as he had felt on any other case in his career. The entire case was to be primarily his responsibility, with Stakely assisting only in the final weeks of preparation and during the trial itself. It was Keene's to win or lose. He was aware from the beginning that, if he lost, he would shoulder the majority of the blame. It was important to him to win because it would have far-reaching implications for the medical community. Our surgical group had been around for thirty-five years and was generally regarded as one of the best in the area, almost a standard of care itself. To lose this case would be damaging to his reputation in the area and would perhaps adversely affect his career. The pressure was particularly intense because he knew that almost any jury would be naturally sympathetic to Kathy, a young mother stricken with cancer at age twenty-six, coping with a colostomy, an amputation, a stroke, and a divorce.

Kathy was being represented by the law firm of Susan Loggans and Associates from Chicago. She had contacted Ms. Loggans after reading an article about her in the August, 1982, issue of *Working Woman*, over a year after her final discharge from the hospital. The article appeared under the "Success Story" section of the magazine and described Ms. Loggans' success as a plaintiff's attorney, noting that she owned three homes in addition to an airplane. Her firm was anticipating a profit-margin of over a million dollars during that year. Perhaps the part of the article that tweaked Kathy's interest was that Ms. Loggans specialized in personal injury cases and had recently won an 8.5 million dollar settlement for a twenty-three-year-old who was paralyzed following an operation. I have often pondered the difference that it might have made in my life if Kathy had overlooked that one little article.

ॐ

The period between the time that a lawsuit is filed and the time it comes to trial is known in the legal profession as the "period of discovery." This is the time that the plaintiff's attorneys (who filed the suit) and the defendant's attorneys attempt to discover what each other will contend at the time of trial. This discovery is done largely through "depositions," which are sworn testimonies taken under oath in the presence of a duly appointed court reporter. The attorneys for each side have an obligation under the law to name in advance witnesses they intend to call to testify at the trial.

They must make the witnesses available to the opposing attorney in order that he might "depose" them and try to discover what they intend to say at the trial. Depositions are crucial in that they are admissable as evidence at the time of the trial. The plaintiff's attorney attempts to get the defendant and his witnesses to be as specific as possible in their depositions. If defendants can be manipulated into saying things that support the plaintiff, these statements can later be introduced at trial, placing the defendant in the uncomfortable position of either standing by those damaging statements or explaining to the jury why they said it before but have now changed their minds. Likewise, the defendant's attorney attempts to do the same with the plaintiff and the plaintiff's witnesses.

It is not unusual for the period of discovery to drag on for more than two years as it did in our case, a lingering cloud of darkness varying in intensity from time to time, but ever-present. Our trial was originally scheduled for September, 1984, then continued (postponed) until March and finally until August, 1985. We were anxious to get the trial behind us and were increasingly frustrated by the delays that seemed to be a way of life for those in the legal profession. Dr. Cameron had to be away from the practice for periods of time in order to help with depositions as far away as Chicago, Illinois, and Sarasota, Florida. There were numerous interruptions in our daily schedules. On one occasion I cancelled my office and surgical schedules to be in Chicago for a deposition, only to have it cancelled without explanation at the last minute.

I never met Susan Loggans (and hope to avoid that dubious distinction in the future), but in July, 1984, a full fifteen months after the suit had been filed, her understudy, Lee DeWald, came to Montgomery to take our depositions. We knew that there was little chance that Mr. DeWald would be aware that *Heparin* was the culprit that caused Kathy's critical illness, her amputation, and her stroke. The "experts" were both retired from active surgical practice and almost surely would not have known about the problems with *Heparin* that were described in the literature. Our preference was that Mr. DeWald remain in the dark concerning those problems until the time of the trial. We had been counseled by Tommy Keene that, whereas we had to tell the truth at all times, we were under no obligation to educate Mr. De-Wald. His own "experts" were responsible for that. We had to answer truthfully all of his questions, but we did not have to elaborate, clarify, or volunteer information. It was Mr. DeWald's job to phrase his questions in such a way that he would discover what we knew.

When I met Mr. DeWald, I was surprised that he appeared to be in his early thirties and had rather boyish features in his rounded face, not at all the imposing figure that I had envisioned to be representing a high-powered Chicago law firm. I realized that I was already thinking like a lawyer as I sized him up to be the kind of person who might not particularly appeal to a jury.

After I had sworn to speak the truth, Mr. DeWald began asking the routine questions related to age, educational background, medical society memberships, and other general questions. When he began to ask specific questions about the care rendered Kathy Roberts, it was obvious by his line of questioning that the thrust of his case was going to be that Kathy developed an infection because the ureter was cut and that the infection had caused her to lose her leg and have a stroke. He did not seem to have the slightest inkling that *Heparin* was in any way related to her problems. However, in the course of going through the hospital record and asking questions about it, he began to ask about her stroke.

"It says 'dense right hemiplegia persists.' What is hemiplegia a result of?" DeWald asked.

"The stroke," I succinctly responded, mindful of Tommy Keene's admonition not to elaborate.

"And do you have an opinion as to how she got her stroke?" he continued.

"Yes," I said, following Tommy's instructions exactly.

"What is your opinion?"

"Clots in the vessels in the brain."

I knew he was on the right trail now. If he followed this line of questioning, I had perhaps one more answer before I would have to specifically acknowledge that it was my opinion that *Heparin* had caused the clotting. As expected, he continued the logical line of questioning.

"And how did she get the clots in the vessels in the brain?" he asked.

"The clotting factors and platelets agglutinate and then plug up the vessels," I responded.

This was indeed what had happened and was the absolutely truthful answer to his question. However, I realized if his next question was "And what caused that?" the only answer that I could give would be *"Heparin."* I decided to take a chance. Immediately on the heels of my previous answer, I asked if I could take a break and get a glass of water. I felt certain Mr. DeWald would see through this ploy and come right back to this line of questioning after the break. Five minutes later when we resumed the deposition, I held my breath while awaiting DeWald's first question. Incredibly, he began an entirely different line of questioning and never came back to the stroke.

I had answered all of his questions truthfully, but I had not educated him. How strange it felt, though, to be playing a game of cat and mouse with Mr. DeWald, fervently seeking to keep him in darkness so that truth might ultimately prevail. I was convinced that truth was on my side, but I was equally convinced that I had to play the game in order to establish that fact. This avoidance of full disclosure is standard in the legal profession. It's the name of the game. It has nothing to do with right or wrong, justice or injustice. It is simply the way things are done by both sides. By promoting this type of behavior, our legal system, whose stated goal is to find truth, has become almost a caricature of itself.

Chapter 9

Believe an expert; believe one
who has had experience.
—St. Bernard of Clairvaux

When George Wallace decided to seek an unprecedented fourth term as governor, the political climate in Alabama had changed considerably from the time when he was elected to his first term. In 1963 when he "stood in the schoolhouse door" to prevent Vivian Malone and James Hood from registering at the University of Alabama, blacks made up only a small percentage of the voters in Alabama. However, in 1980, as a result of the 1965 Voting Rights Act and the subsequent voter registration drives, the number of black voters had increased substantially, making them a voting force with which to be reckoned. Wallace, a consummate politician with uncanny political savvy, realized that he could not win the election without strong black support. He orchestrated a clever campaign to convince black voters that he was no longer the arch segregationist they had known in the sixties, but rather the champion of black causes — their hope for the future. And it worked. He received a majority of the black vote and won the election. During the campaign he had made some pledges to appoint blacks to various political offices, and he needed to fulfill those pledges — at least in a token way.

Charles Price never dreamed as a boy that he would one day become circuit judge in his home town of Montgomery, Alabama. He grew up in the forties and fifties, a "Negro" in a thoroughly segregated society with all of its inherent social and cultural deprivations. The product of a "broken home," he and his family survived on the income his mother earned as a maid in a local hotel. Statistically it would have been far more likely for young Charles to eventually end up in a court of law charged with some crime rather than sitting on a bench deciding the fate of criminals, both black and white. His mother, however, instilled in him the value of honesty, integrity, and hard work; and those values eventually paid handsome dividends.

After serving his country in the 82nd Airborne Division of the U. S. Army and graduating from Virginia Union University, Charles Price graduated with honors from George Washington University Law School. Following a brief tenure with the United States Justice Department, he returned to Alabama and became an Assistant Attorney General.

Later he became a top prosecutor in the Montgomery County District Attorney's office, establishing a reputation that eventually led to his appointment as a municipal judge. He was thus in the right place at the right time to be appointed a circuit court judge by Wallace in 1983.

Our trial was randomly assigned to Judge Price's court, an assignment that troubled our attorneys somewhat. We would have liked the opportunity to use Dr. Hamp Greene, the neurologist who treated Kathy in the hospital, as a witness. He had already testified in deposition that he thought Kathy had received excellent care, that her blood was clotting abnormally, and that her stroke was caused by a blood vessel having been plugged up. The hematologist and the pulmonary specialist would have been valuable experts for us as well. There was also an infectious disease specialist who had moved to town subsequent to Kathy's hospitalization who had reviewed her chart and found her care to be excellent, including discontinuance of antibiotics on the second postoperative day. The problem with all of these potential witnesses was that they were insured, as we were, by the Mutual Assurance Society of Alabama. Their testimony would at least theoretically be prejudiced by the knowledge that a verdict against the defendant would mean higher insurance rates for all doctors insured by the company, including their own. Judge Price, in previous cases, had ruled that if the defendant called expert witnesses who were insured by the same company as they, the plaintiff's attorney could point out to the jury a potential conflict of interest, and in so doing inform the jury that they had millions of dollars in insurance coverage. Our attorneys were strongly opposed to allowing Kathy's attorneys to wave this flag in the face of the jurors. I assumed that all jurors would know that we had malpractice insurance coverage, but Tommy and Charlie

thought it was crucial that we not let that be directly pointed
out to them. The ordinary juror does not realize that the
money awarded to plaintiffs ultimately comes from the
pockets of all members of society. Whether the defendant is
a physician, a business, a manufacturer of products, or a
municipality, the loss must be passed along to the consumer
in the form of an increase in the cost of goods and services.
When a juror mistakenly believes that the money will come
from a large insurance company and will have little effect on
the remainder of society, there is a tendency to want to
award the unfortunate victim large sums of money, regardless
of the facts in the case.

To get around the problem of allowing Kathy's attorneys
to tell the jury that we had millions of dollars in insurance
coverage, we needed to use expert witnesses who were
covered by some other insurance company. The physicians
at the University of Alabama Medical Center had their own
self-insurance plan and were not covered by Mutual Assurance. We could therefore use experts from there without fear
of introducing insurance coverage into the case. Charlie was
aware of a young surgeon there, Dr. James Orr, whom neither
Dr. Cameron nor I had ever met. His specialty was pelvic
cancer surgery in women — an ideally qualified witness in the
case. Charlie contacted Dr. Orr who graciously agreed to review the long detailed record. After his review, he was in-
censed that anyone was being sued after providing such high-
quality care. He approached the case like a zealot with a
cause, carefully examining the minutiae in the records and
finding things that supported our case that even we had
missed in our reviews. He volunteered to have the medical
illustration department at the University prepare large color
drawings of the female pelvis to allow the jury to better
understand the operation.

During my residency at the University Hospital in Birmingham, I had the privilege of studying under Dr. William Maddox, one of the premier cancer surgeons in the United States. Widely respected in his field, he maintains an unassuming humility that engenders immediate respect from anyone who encounters him. I knew that he would make an excellent witness and asked our lawyers to contact him. His first question after being briefed about the case was, "when did she die?" He, too, was incredulous that she was alive almost five years later and was suing those who were, in large part, responsible for her recovery. We had a problem with using Dr. Maddox, however. Although he was on the faculty at the Medical Center, he was actually in private practice in Birmingham and was insured by Mutual Assurance. As the trial date approached and Kathy's attorneys had not even bothered to obtain depositions from either of our expert witnesses, Tommy and Charlie decided that in all likelihood Dr. Maddox's insurance company had not been researched, and the plaintiff's attorneys would assume he was covered by the University contract. We deemed his testimony important enough to take the chance, and the gamble worked. The issue of insurance never came up during the trial.

Chapter 10

*No man prospers so suddenly
as by other's errors.*
—Francis Bacon

A s the months passed, some interesting things were going on with the plaintiff's attorneys. Kathy had originally contacted Susan Loggans and Associates law firm in Chicago, and her case had been turned over to young Lee DeWald. The Chicago lawyers had apparently enlisted the help of Ben Hogan III, of Birmingham, in filing the suit because the original summons was filed jointly by Loggans' firm and Hogan's firm. Hogan was apparently actively involved in the early stages of the case but in October, 1983, withdrew from the case and substituted Howard Mandell, a Montgomery attorney, to aid the Loggans firm. Unfortunately, it was not the last that we would hear from Mr. Hogan.

Before a malpractice suit can go to trial, the plaintiff must have an "expert witness" who, by virtue of his education and experience, possesses knowledge not commonly known to the laity and agrees with the plaintiff that the standard of care has been breached. By January, 1985, the only expert witness Lee DeWald had was Dr. Hyman Lans, a semi-retired Chicago surgeon who had not done a major operation in over five years. Since 1979 he had supplemented his income by reviewing medical records for plaintiffs' attorneys, primarily Mr. DeWald and his firm. Dr. Lans charges $150 an hour to review records, $225 an hour for depositions, which usually last several hours, and $1500 a day plus travel expenses to appear in court. He was in Montgomery three days for our trial. He acknowledged reviewing at least twenty to twenty-five records during the last few years and claimed to have spent portions of eight to ten days on Kathy's records alone. Simple arithmetic reveals that this is a rather lucrative way of supplementing one's income.

In November, 1984, Dr. Lans reviewed Kathy's chart and the depositions Mr. DeWald had taken from Dr. Cameron and me the previous July. Dr. Lans subsequently wrote a letter to Mr. DeWald outlining what he would be able to tell a jury were instances of negligence. A copy of that letter was made available to Tommy Keene who, in turn, made it available to Dr. Cameron and me. Dr. Lans' opinion expressed in the letter was that "the dividing of the right ureter was below the usual standard of surgical care." He further noted that "the failure to have a urological consultation prior to May 1, 1981, in spite of urinary drainage, elevated temperature, and tachycardia were incidents of substandard medical care by Dr. Snider. . . ." When I read that, I realized for the first time that I was not involved in the lawsuit only because I helped Dr. Cameron with the operation. There were, indeed, going to be allegations that my care of Kathy was negligent. My first reaction was one of embarrassment at having my care called negligent by another physician. After reviewing the record again my embarrassment gave way to anger. The temperature and tachycardia (rapid pulse) that he referred to were, in fact, normal postoperative levels that almost all patients have after major surgery. And why in the name of Heaven did Dr. Lans consider it negligent to not have a urologist following her that week? There was nothing for a urologist to do at that time. Did he think a urologist would have done anything different that week and, if so, pray tell, what?

In January, 1985, Tommy Keene and John Cameron went to Chicago and, with Mr. DeWald present, obtained Dr. Lans' deposition. Mr. DeWald was apparently not completely happy with his "expert's" performance because he then began to search for additional experts and, in February, 1985, contacted Dr. Richard Williams in Sarasota, Florida.

Dr. Williams would be considered by some to be a quintessential "hired gun" in the malpractice business. He and his son had been practicing surgeons in Warsaw, New York, a town of about for thousand inhabitants. Four malpractice suits were filed against the two surgeons in a relatively brief period of time, and both of them left town on the same day. The elder Dr. Williams moved to Sarasota and attempted to become licensed to practice medicine. Unable to pass the state licensing exam, he began to review medical records and testify against physicians in malpractice cases. He advertised his services to plaintiffs' attorneys in *Trial* magazine and soon had a booming business. He got referrals from various groups and corporations set up specifically to obtain "expert" witnesses for malpractice cases. His referrals initially came from a group in Reston, Virginia, euphemistically known as Medical Quality Foundation, but later from such places as Baileys Crossroads, Virginia; Tampa, Florida; Willoughby, Ohio; and El Cajun, California. By his own estimation he had given around fifty depositions in the last few years and had testified in court four or five times in Alabama. At the time Tommy Keene and John Cameron went to Sarasota for his deposition in May, 1985, he estimated that he had around a hundred cases pending on his shelf.

Dr. Williams' deposition must have been a bewildering experience for Lee DeWald. Despite trying to help him in every way possible, Dr. Williams said a number of things that were damaging to his case. One of the things Dr. Lans had said in his deposition was that we should have had a urologist actually repair the damaged ureter. Dr. Williams testified that he had no criticism at all of the fact that Dr. Cameron had repaired the ureter and that he had repaired ureters himself as a general surgeon. He said that he thought it was a perfectly acceptable area within which a general surgeon could perform and that he thought the ureter was repaired appropriately. Perhaps even more damaging was his testimony that he didn't know why Kathy had had a stroke but that it was not a recognized complication of phlebitis and that "you can't get emboli from the leg to the brain." He further agreed that phlebitis is a common problem after surgery — that even "a simple hernia repair has a high incidence of thrombophlebitis" and that Kathy could have had phlebitis from day one.

These two retired surgeons, Dr. Lans and Dr. Williams, neither of whom had done a major operation nor taken care of a critically ill patient in years, were the "experts" who would weigh us in the balance and find us wanting. It seemed unjust.

Almost two years to the day after the lawsuit was originally filed, DeWald finally got around to taking the deposition of Dr. Tim Morrow, the urologist who treated Kathy and whom Mr. DeWald and Dr. Lans thought should have been involved in her care sooner. According to Dr. Morrow's testimony at the deposition, even if he had been following her all along he would not have altered her treatment. He testified that the ureter had been repaired correctly and that he had done an x-ray in December, 1981, that showed a normal kidney, indicating that she had sustained no permanent injury as a result of the severed ureter. He testified that he would have given antibiotics only for two or three days and then stopped them in order to prevent the development of resistant strains of bacteria. Finally, when Mr. De-Wald asked him if the phlebitis could have been caused by the leak from the ureter his response was, "No, absolutely not. . . . I just don't see the relationship."

DeWald must have realized that his case was crumbling before his very eyes. I was scheduled to go to Chicago to assist Tommy Keene in obtaining the deposition of another "expert" witness about that same time, but that deposition was abruptly cancelled at the last minute. Lee DeWald and the Susan Loggans and Associates law firm withdrew from the case a few weeks later.

Chapter 11

June-August, 1985

In all things, success depends upon
previous preparation, and without
such preparation there is sure to be
failure.
—Confucius

he news that the Chicago lawyers had dropped
the case gave us an optimistic hope that the suit
would be dropped entirely without our having to
go through the ordeal of a week-long trial with
our names splattered daily in the newspapers. We knew that

there was very little likelihood that a newspaper reporter was going to get the facts involved in this case straight enough to communicate to the people of Montgomery what had actually transpired. We also knew that many people would judge us guilty merely because we were charged with malpractice. Our hopes for a dismissal were short-lived. We were informed that Ben Hogan, the same Birmingham attorney who had assisted with the filing of the case two years earlier, was back on the case. When the Loggans firm withdrew, Hogan interviewed Kathy, apparently concluded she might be able to sway a jury, and decided to give it a try. And why shouldn't he? The major expense of the case had already been borne by the Loggans firm. All Hogan had to do was invest a few thousand dollars to get Dr. Lans to come from Chicago, take a week off himself to come to Montgomery, and roll the dice. It was perhaps a longshot that he would win; but if he got the right jury, he could possibly go home a few hundred thousand dollars richer.

We had named our experts long before and had offered to make them available for deposition. DeWald had never gotten around to deposing them, and now Hogan would not have time to do so before the trial. An essential part of adequate preparation for a trial is to depose the opponent's witnesses and know exactly what they intend to say before getting into the courtroom. Hogan was going to go to trial without deposing either of our experts and without having the foggiest notion how they were likely to respond to his questions in front of the jury. I could not help believing the medical care Kathy received was infinitely better than the legal care she was getting.

The Friday before our trial began, Dr. Cameron and I and our other partners took the afternoon off to meet with Tommy and Charlie to go over our final preparations. Dr.

Cameron and I favored a direct approach with the jury — trying to tell them exactly what had happened. At the time we were treating Kathy we didn't completely understand everything that happened to her, but we thought one of the most likely explanations was that she was septic, even though that could not account for all of her problems. Dr. Cameron signed the discharge summary reflecting that theory because it was the best explanation we had at the time. Subsequently, several articles had been published in the literature describing similar patients and, in retrospect, we were able to understand that the problem had not been sepsis at all but a rare allergy to *Heparin*. Tommy and Charlie insisted that we not be so adamant in telling the jury that we understood now what we did not understand then. They had several strong objections to that candid approach. First and foremost, the jury was not going to be able to follow it if we started talking about too many technical things. Second, they were afraid Hogan would contend that we had changed our story, not because of our new-found knowledge, but because we were being sued — that we were trying to "cover up" the facts in the case that we had previously recorded in black and white. Finally, they didn't want to come down too strongly on the fact that her problems were related to a drug that we had given her, because Hogan might try to convince the jury that we should have known about *Heparin* allergies and been able to do something about it. We argued with Tommy and Charlie that this case had taken place in 1981, and we could produce authoritative texts published years after this with no mention of thrombosis being related to *Heparin*. Hogan's own experts apparently were unaware of it in 1985. Why should we have been expected to be omniscient in 1981?

Dr. Cameron and I were still laboring under the erroneous

assumption that a jury would not have totally unreasonable expectations of a physician. Unfortunately, that is not always the case. Gail Kalmowitz, for example, was born prematurely in 1952. Soon thereafter she developed blindness from a disease called retrolental fibroplasia, the cause of which was unknown at the time. In 1956 it was established that the cause of blindness in premature infants was actually the high concentrations of oxygen given to save their lives. The study which established that fact was not even begun until three months after Gail's birth — long after the damage had been done to her eyes. In 1975, however, she sued the hospital and the doctors who had "caused" her blindness, even though the care she had received was the standard for the time. The case was tried and went to the jury. Minutes before they were to return their verdict, Gail, afraid she was about to lose, accepted a settlement of $165,000. The jury was going to return a verdict in her favor of $900,000. It was clearly a case in which the sympathy of the jury caused them to ignore the medical evidence of the case and return an emotional verdict.

Understandably, our arguments to Tommy and Charlie concerning the general state of knowledge of *Heparin* allergies in 1981 fell on deaf ears. Whereas we were trying to vindicate ourselves, Tommy and Charlie were trying to win the verdict by putting together a simple case that the jury could both understand and believe. They knew how juries thought and behaved. They worked with juries for a living. We had never faced one. Ultimately, we reluctantly bowed to their judgment. We agreed to acknowledge that she still possibly could have had sepsis, but if she did, it was a recognized complication of this type of surgery and it was appropriately treated.

Dr. Cameron and I went to our attorneys' office and

worked all Saturday morning and into the afternoon with them, going over our plans again and again. They tried to anticipate every question we would be asked so that we would have a minimum of surprises on the witness stand. They even asked questions designed to make us angry so they could see how we would react. They coached us in facial expression, body language, and tone of voice, instructing us to speak distinctly and confidently and to get eye contact with the jurors.

After we left their office, Tommy and Charlie worked the remainder of the afternoon and into the night. They returned on Sunday and continued their preparations. Their philosophy was that they were not adequately prepared unless they had anticipated everything that could possibly come up during the trial. They assumed that their opponent would be exceedingly bright and exceedingly thorough, and they consequently planned for many things that never came up. Perhaps it was overkill, but it helped to relieve my apprehension.

I spent the remainder of the weekend reviewing Kathy's thick hospital record, the stack of depositions, and the pertinent medical literature one more time. I could quote most of it in my sleep by now. I was confident that we were as prepared as we possibly could be, and I was ready and eager to get on with it.

Chapter 12

Monday morning, August 26, 1985

> *A man should be tried by a*
> *jury of his peers.*
> —Goethe

On Monday morning Dr. Cameron and I drove to the courthouse together. I could sense in his voice that he was as nervous as I at the prospect of beginning this alien ordeal. I had watched the lawsuit take its inexorable toll on him for some time now. Ordinarily possessed with a supreme confidence in his knowledge and abilities, there had been times lately when he seemed unsure of himself. In the nine years that I had known him and worked with him on a daily basis in one of life's most stressful professions, only the death of his wife had shaken his serene tranquility more than this lawsuit. It seemed so unfair that this man who had given so much of himself to his patients, while asking for so little in return was being tormented like this.

We arrived at the courthouse shortly after 8:30 and found Tommy Keene and Charlie Stakely already there. They had gone to their office about six o'clock that morning to go over the final details of preparation. As usual, before going to trial, they had spent essentially the entire weekend in the office preparing. Their success in defending malpractice cases probably lies in their belief that they don't have to outsmart the plaintiff's attorney, just out-prepare him. It is not at all uncommon to find them in their office at five in the morning or at ten at night, painstakingly poring over the minute details of the case, playing the devil's advocate with each other, anticipating everything that might come up in the trial. The acquittal of their clients is of the utmost importance to each of them and takes priority over almost everything else in their lives around the time of the trial.

Dr. Cameron and I entered a side door to the courtroom and walked to the far side where Tommy and Charlie were sitting. The room was not quite as big as I had pictured it in my mind. The back half contained five rows of unpadded wooden pews divided by a center aisle, not at all unlike what one would find in a small country church. The families and friends tend to arrange themselves on the side of the room of either the plaintiff or the defendant, as in a wedding, depending on whom they are supporting. The spectators' half of the room was separated from the participants' half by a three-foot wooden rail. Inside the rail, in front of the imposing judge's bench was a U-shaped table with the limbs directed toward the bench. I surmised that the gentleman thumbing through papers at the opposite end of the table must be Hogan. He looked a little more distinguished than DeWald, and I silently wished Lee were still on the case. On the side of the room nearest Hogan was the jury section, also enclosed by a short rail. At the end of the judge's bench nearest the jury was the witness stand. I noticed a microphone there and felt my pulse quicken. I had not anticipated speaking into a microphone, and for some reason it made me a little more nervous.

I had not seen Kathy for over four years; but when she walked in, I recognized her immediately. I was strangely relieved that she was still quite overweight.   Perhaps, I thought, the jury will realize how difficult it is to operate on people her size. She walked with a slight limp because of her artificial leg, but had no visible evidence of any impairment from her stroke. She avoided eye contact with me as she came over and sat three feet to my left. I wondered if she felt any embarrassment over dragging us through this ordeal. I could not fathom how anyone could sue a person who had done his level best and saved her life, without feeling at least a twinge of embarrassment when seeing him face-to-face.

The chairs were arranged around the table such that Tommy was sitting in the middle of our end of the table, directly facing the jury across the wide expanse of the table. He was flanked by Charlie, nearest the judge, and Dr. Cameron on the other side. I sat around the corner of the table from Dr. Cameron, facing the judge. Kathy sat next to me, with Hogan and his assistant sitting on the other side of her, nearest the jury.

Just before nine, about sixty jurors filed into the room
and sat in the spectators' section. Tommy and Charlie craned
their necks to study the candidates as they walked in, observing them for anything that might give a clue as to what
kind of jurors they were likely to be.

Shortly after nine, Judge Price walked out of his chambers
through a door behind the bench. I was surprised that no
one formally announced his arrival. No one even stood up
the way they do in the movies or on television. He did wear
a long, black robe over his short stocky frame and signaled
the opening of court with a rap from an official looking gav-
el. The judge began by explaining to the jurors that this was
to be a case involving an allegation of medical malpractice
and that he would be asking a series of questions (known as
the *voir dire*) to determine if any of the potential jurors
should be disqualified because of bias. The attorneys for
each side listen to the responses and then have a limited opportunity to ask further questions of their own in order to
make their decisions concerning whom to "strike" or eliminate. Neither attorney can select a juror. They can only
strike potential jurors they definitely do not want to serve.
This is done in an alternating manner until fourteen remain,
two of whom are alternates who would deliberate only in the
event that a regular juror became unable to serve during the
course of the trial. The jurors do not know who among them
are alternates until they are ready to retire to deliberate so
that the alternates will retain an equal interest in the testimony.

Judge Price asked each of the future jurors to stand and
give his name and occupation. He then went through a long
series of questions concerning their backgrounds related to
medical care or previous lawsuits. He asked whether anyone
would find it difficult to rule either in favor of or against a

physician due to some prejudice. He specifically asked if a juror or a family member had had a bad experience with a doctor or a hospital. No one acknowledged any such experience. (I wondered at the time if a person who had had a bad experience might not be tempted to withhold that information in order to get on the jury and have an opportunity to vicariously retaliate.) The judge asked if anyone had been treated by Dr. Cameron or me but did not ask about our partners. Hogan also failed in his follow-up to ask that important question.

After the questioning was completed, we were allowed to retire to anterooms for about twenty minutes to discuss the upcoming strikes. I was amazed at the recall Tommy and Charlie had for what potential jurors looked like, where they worked, and what they had said. Tommy and Charlie realized that the decision they were about to make could win or lose the case. Tommy began going down the list and arranging two groups — those that he must strike, and those that he would like to strike if possible. We had to cover about sixty people in twenty minutes, which left no more than twenty seconds of discussion for each.

We wanted to have a jury that was as educated and intelligent as possible. It was going to be difficult for even the most erudite non-medical person to follow the facts of the case, but we were confident that we could win if the jury made a decision based upon an understanding of the facts. With this in mind, some of the decisions our attorneys made surprised me. There were a couple of uneducated people that I thought they would want to strike for sure. However, they sized them up as jurors who would not express an opinion one way or another, but would go along with the flow of the majority. "Fillers," they called them. They would not waste strikes on them but use their strikes to eliminate jurors whom they thought would be ruled by emotion and sympathy for the plaintiff rather than by reason and a determination to discover the truth.

We returned to the courtroom, and the process of striking the jury commenced. Hogan went first and struck a rehabilitation counselor who had obvious physical handicaps which were worse than Kathy's. He had been on our possible strike list because we were not certain how his handicaps would affect his sympathy for Kathy. Hogan apparently was afraid he would not be sympathetic since he had obviously overcome the hardships life had dealt him and was a productive member of society.

Tommy and Charlie studied their list, thought a minute, whispered to each other, then deliberately made their first strike. Almost without hesitation, Hogan made his second strike. So it went, alternating back and forth, with Hogan quickly striking his and Keene deliberating before making his strikes until there were only fourteen remaining. They were calling out only the jurors' numbers and not their names, so I was not certain until it was said and done who was left on the jury. Hogan apparently had a list arranged that he went through in a predetermined order. Keene and Stakely weighed each of Hogan's strikes to see where he was going before making their next strike, almost like a quarterback calling his next play audibly at the line of scrimmage after seeing how his opponent is lined up.

When the striking process ended, the fourteen remaining jurors filed into the jury box and were seated. I was astounded to see that an articulate young woman, who had identified herself as knowing both Keene and Stakely from church, was on the jury. Another woman Hogan had left had been operated upon by one of our other partners who was still seeing her regularly in follow-up. I was happy to see a young medical technician had survived the striking process. Though I did not know her, I thought her experience in the medical field would enable her to interpret some of the medical problems to the other jurors.

Four of the jurors were male: a university professor, a Navy recruiter, a tire changer, and a retiree. The last had a kind face and seemed to be the type of person who would genuinely try to do what was just and right, but I wondered how well he would follow the case and how forceful he would be in his opinion. The Navy recruiter dressed and carried himself in a manner that would best be described in the vernacular as "laid back." He would saunter in at the last minute each day, and appeared, in general, quite bored with the whole process. His behavior caused us some degree of consternation. The tire changer had responded in the *voir dire* that he had served on a jury in a malpractice case before. Hogan did not ask and, therefore, did not know that he had returned a verdict for the defendant in a case defended by Keene several years earlier and would probably have little trouble doing so again. Unfortunately, he misunderstood the judge's instruction one day and failed to return after lunch for the afternoon session, relegating himself to an alternate status. We were apprehensive about the white professor who taught at a predominantly black university. This university affiliation, combined with his full beard, caused Tommy and Charlie to worry that he might be "antiestablishment" and therefore more sympathetic to the plaintiff than to the physicians. He had been on our possible strike list, but we had to accept him. I was intrigued with him the entire week. He was obviously intelligent and paid careful attention to every word that was said, taking rather frequent notes. He remained absolutely poker-faced the entire time and never gave any clues about what he was thinking.

There was only one juror whom I felt relatively secure in "reading" during the week. Several months earlier I had culminated two and one-half years of night school and had received a master's degree in counseling. Part of what I had learned was to observe people for non-verbal clues as to what they were thinking. A break in eye contact, a fleeting smile, a raised eyebrow, a frown, or a sigh can communicate what is going on inside a person. I had pegged one young female data processor as being on "our side." I was certain from her smiles and her eye contact that she was "with us," and I told Tommy and Charlie after I testified that I was certain we had her vote.

There was a sweet little lady on the back row who resembled my mother. Irrational as it seemed, that resemblance did give me a little comfort and security.

Tommy and Charlie were concerned about a middle-aged black woman whose husband owned a funeral home. I was not certain what their concern was, but they had been unable to strike her, and, because they were worried, I was worried. I was far more apprehensive, though, about a young licensed practical nurse who worked at a local nursing home. I surmised that those nurses might not see the highest quality of medical care, and I wondered how that might affect her viewpoint. It was hard to put a finger on it, but there was something in her demeanor that made me wonder if she had an unacknowledged bias.

Of the three remaining women, the only other one from whom I got any bad vibrations was a Pizza Hut waitress. She and the LPN seemed to be pals, and they emitted similar vibrations.

These were the people who would decide our fate. Charlie leaned over and quietly asked if it looked like a jury of my peers. It did not. I believe very deeply in the worth and the value of each individual, and I certainly do not think that I am any better than any of the men and women who served on that jury. But in this case a jury of my peers would be composed of people who could understand the intricacies of the medical issues involved. It would be twelve people who have stood in my shoes making those difficult decisions when a person's life hangs in the balance, decisions made with no crystal ball to predict the future and without the luxury of retrospectively reviewing the case when the outcome is already known. It would be people who knew what Hippocrates was writing about when he wrote of how perilous this experience may be in the art of medicine, and how fleeting the moments are when difficult decisions must be made.

I do not believe the authors of our Constitution ever intended for a Pizza Hut waitress and a tire changer and a Navy recruiter to decide whether a physician's treatment was within the "standard of care." The jury system was adopted to settle disputes which ordinary laymen could understand and judge, whether someone had stolen a neighbor's cattle or built a fence on another's land, not whether the cause of a cerebral vascular accident was related to thrombosis produced by platelet agglutination from an immune response to an anticoagulant.

But, like it or not, our task was to try to teach in five days things that had taken us more than thirteen years to learn.

Chapter 13

> *A lie which is all a lie may be met and fought*
> *with outright, but a lie which is part a truth*
> *is a harder matter to fight.*
> —Tennyson

After the jury was selected and sworn in, Judge Price issued an unusual ruling. According to the law, any witness who is to testify in a case is not allowed to sit in and listen to preceding testimony. Judge Price ruled that Dr. Hyman Lans, Hogan's witness from Chicago, was exempt from this rule and could sit in on all of the testimony given prior to the time that he took the stand. This ruling would obviously give Dr. Lans (and Hogan) a tremendous advantage and seemed a bit unfair from my perspective. The purpose of the law is to insure that witnesses testify based on their knowledge of the facts, unbiased by the testimony of others. I could see no logical reason why Dr. Lans should be an exception to the rule.

After making this ruling, Judge Price began his instructions to the jury. "Now ladies and gentlemen, you all have been selected to serve as a jury in the matter of Kathy Roberts versus Dr. John Cameron and Dr. Howard C. Snider. As I stated to you earlier, I am going to let the lawyers in their opening statements tell you mainly what this case is all about, but let me briefly tell you the procedure by which this case will be tried. The plaintiff is represented by Attorney Ben Hogan, the gentleman sitting closest to you. The plaintiff is the lady in the blue suit, Ms. Roberts, who filed the lawsuit and stated certain allegations. She sued Dr. Cameron, the gentleman in the gray suit, and Dr. Snider, the gentleman in the blue suit to his left. They are the defendants in the case and are represented by Attorneys Charles Stakely and Thomas Keene. Now these lawyers have a duty to present their side of the case as vigorously and competently as they have been trained.

"I am Judge Price and my duty is to rule on questions of law and to make sure that the case moves along in an orderly fashion. I will be dealing with what the lawyers are doing and any objections they make. If I should sustain an objection, that means the witness cannot answer that question and if the witness does answer that question, then you are to disregard that answer. If I should overrule an objection, that means that the witness can answer that question. At the appropriate time you will go into the jury room, all twelve of you together, and reach a verdict. You will do that based on the evidence that you have heard and the law that is applicable in this case.

"The evidence in this case will come from the witness stand — it will be up to you to decide the credibility of the witnesses and what weight you want to put on their testimony — and any other documents that I admit into this trial. The questions by the lawyers are not evidence in the case. Any rulings I make from the bench, sustain, overrule, whatever I say to the lawyers, is not evidence in the case and you are not to be persuaded by that one way or the other. There will be times during this trial that I have to go back in chambers with the lawyers and take care of the matters back there. Now, when I do that, I am not trying to hide anything or keep anything from you, but the law says there are certain things I must make an independent ruling on first, before I decide whether or not to allow you to hear or see it.

"Now the case will be tried as follows: Mr. Hogan will be given an opportunity — since he represents the plaintiff and the plaintiff has the burden of proving to you by a preponderance of the evidence, to your reasonable satisfaction, the truth of her allegations — to give you the first part of his opening statement. When he finishes, Mr. Stakely and Mr. Keene will give you their opening statement. Then Mr. Hogan, of course, comes back and rebuts what they say if he deems it necessary. After that, they will call witnesses.

"At the end of the trial, Mr. Hogan will be given the opportunity to give you the opening part of his closing statement. Mr. Stakely and Mr. Keene will give you their closing statement, and Mr. Hogan will come back and rebut what they say at that point, if he deems it necessary. After that, I will charge you on the law that is applicable in this case, and then you will go into the jury room and reach your verdict. Until the time that I charge you on the law and you go into the jury room, don't discuss the case with anyone and don't allow anyone to discuss the case with you. You have to make up your mind independently on what you have heard."

When Judge Price had finished his initial instructions to the jury, he asked Mr. Hogan to give his opening statement and instructed the jury that they were free to make notes.

Hogan introduced himself and his associate, Ron Cook, who had been to law school but had not yet passed the bar exam. He explained to the jury that in a civil case such as this, his burden was to reasonably satisfy the jurors that his side of the case was more likely true than the defendant's side. He did not have to prove his case beyond a reasonable doubt to a moral certainty, as it would be if this were a criminal case. He had with him a little diagram of the scale of justice, and illustrated to the jury that if he tipped the scale slightly, with fifty-one percent of the evidence, then he would win. He then continued his statement to the jury.

"In a surgical procedure a doctor has a plan. He has step one, step two, step three. But in step sixteen of this procedure, Dr. Cameron was supposed to and did, in fact, isolate out or dissect out, they call it, this tube called the ureter. You are supposed to separate out these ureters in step sixteen of this procedure. He did that. And then in step seventeen, eighteen and nineteen he cut it anyway. He just cut it right in two. The ureter didn't have any cancer in it. He was in there to do some cancer surgery, and he was taking some cancer out from down here, in the colon and the vagina. As part of the procedure, because of just simple carelessness — that's all it was — he cut the ureter. And we are saying that this was a failure to follow the surgical procedure — carelessness, negligence."

It was difficult to sit there and listen to this man who had probably never been in an operating room before describe to the jury how simple things should have been. To him it was easy. You just follow the steps in the book and everything turns out just right. Piece of cake. Literally hundreds of times I have been in the operating room "up to my ass in alligators" attempting to find a ureter, or a nerve, or an artery bound in a thicket of scar tissue and thought how just it would be if Ben Hogan, or Howard Mandell, or any of the other trial lawyers had to be there to help find the hidden structure. Perhaps things would seem less clear and less easy to them under those circumstances. I have fantasized being able to magically grant them the education and experience to be able to do the difficult procedures, then stand back and watch them sweat. It is traumatic enough to have the realization that, if you are less than perfect, your patient may die. Add the fear of a lawsuit and it becomes intolerable.

"The second thing that happened that led to this result," Hogan continued, "is that primarily Dr. Snider (because Dr. Cameron had left her in the care of Dr. Snider, his younger partner) failed to follow and treat infection following the repair of the ureter. Now, I will tell you what the case is not about. First of all there is not going to be any issue that Dr. Cameron and Dr. Snider know the surgical procedure and they have done it many times without any problems. So this is not a matter of where we are saying they are incompetent or they don't know what to do. They do know what to do. Here they were careless."

Hogan seemed to be saying that anytime a ureter is unintentionally cut, it is the result of carelessness. Following his logic, if one is always vigilant and always careful, things will always turn out right. By simply always being careful we can achieve perfection. How much easier the life of a surgeon would be if this were the case. I hoped that the jurors saw the fallacy in his logic. I suspected Hogan did, too, but he had to convince them that we were careless in order to win his case.

"Cancer patients are entitled to the same quality of medical care as other patients," continued Hogan. "Just because somebody has cancer is no excuse to give them any less quality treatment. Finally, postoperative care — and this is something I expect everyone to agree to, Dr. Cameron will agree, Dr. Snider will agree, all of their witnesses will agree — postoperative care is just as important as surgery in the well-being of a patient."

Hogan went on and explained to the jury exactly what constitutes malpractice. He told them that what he had to prove was that the care we delivered fell below the standard set by our peers — that what we did was not in any book, or that it was in the book to do exactly the opposite. After explaining briefly the nature of the operation that was done in January, Hogan went on to talk about the surgery in April.

"What we are talking about is the second surgery. While removing the rest of the cancer, Dr. Cameron severs the right ureter. He isolates it out, knows it's there, and he cuts it anyway. That's what happened. There is no question that's what happened. They won't deny that. He sews it back together. Now here is the part that will have a lot of time devoted to it in the case, because here is a patient who has a repaired, severed ureter, in addition to having had the cancer surgery. She has what's called a Jackson-Pratt drain in her. There are probably a couple of you who know what that is. It's just a drain. 'JP drain' it will show in the hospital records. It goes from inside there, near where that repaired

ureter lies. They stuck a drain inside her body to collect anything that might be leaking from that damaged ureter, after
it was sewn back together, and put it outside her body.
In the hospital records you will see that there was drainage,
constant increasing drainage of urine from the Jackson-
Pratt drain, which means it was coming from the leaking repaired ureter. You understand urine comes from the kidney
down to the bladder and then from the bladder on out of
the body. Now urine collected from where this Jackson-
Pratt drain was was not coming from the bladder. This was
coming from the ureter which was way up here above the
bladder, between the kidneys," said Hogan, pointing to a
drawing that he had in order to illustrate what he was saying.
"So, you'll see that there was a Jackson-Pratt drain removing urine leaking into the body from the repaired ureter. Dr.
Cameron, after surgery, had gone to Europe."

During the time that Kathy was hospitalized, Dr. Cameron's beautiful, talented young wife, Nadia, was herself dying
of colon cancer. Her last request was that he take her to
France one time before she died. He honored that deathbed
request and they left two days after Kathy's operation, returning a week later. Nadia checked into the hospital almost
immediately upon her return, and three weeks later she was
dead. Hogan, of course, did not mention the reason for Dr.
Cameron's trip to Europe.

"Dr. Snider, during these crucial days, was watching —
supposed to be watching — Kathy," he continued.

I felt a surge of anger as Hogan condescendingly sneered
that I was *supposed* to be watching Kathy. I knew that
I could not allow that anger to show. Tommy had drilled
into us that Hogan would intentionally try to make us angry,
and that we had to keep our cool at all costs.

"Snider allows the order for antibiotics to run out April

25. Here is what happens. Dr. Cameron, when he leaves for Europe after the surgery, one of the important orders that he left was for antibiotics to run for three days. Snider comes in on the third day and gave a verbal order to cancel and stop the antibiotics. Now, he then doesn't culture the drain for bacteria. Here we have a drain coming from a severed ureter. You will see when you hear this testimony and see these medical records and even the medical text-books, that urine is not supposed to be draining into the inside of the body. I mean, that's not supposed to be what happens and when it's there, it's a source of infection. So, knowing that this draining inside the body of urine is going on, Dr. Snider not only cancels the antibiotics, but he doesn't even culture."

Hogan then went on to give a somewhat erroneous explanation of what a culture is, confusing it with a gram stain. (A culture is a procedure in which a portion of body fluid is taken to the laboratory and placed on a special gel upon which any bacteria present in the fluid will grow and be identified. A gram stain is a procedure in which the bacteria are smeared on a slide, stained and looked at under the microscope for identification.)

"He doesn't culture the bacteria and ignores signs of infection. Signs of infection include the fact that this drainage was increasing instead of getting less, and she had a spiking temperature. The temperature, as you will see, was going like this." Hogan indicated by waving his finger wildly that her temperature was going way up and way down. "The textbooks say that's a sign of infection. So he ignores the signs of infection. He doesn't culture any, and he stops the antibiotics."

It was becoming increasingly difficult for me to sit still without revealing my incredulity at what Hogan was saying.

The increased drainage did not in any way remotely suggest infection, yet he was calling it a sign of infection. Equally as bad, he was saying that she had a spiking temperature. Her temperature during that week was exactly what one would expect after an operation like she had, but because it varied a little during the day, as fever always does, he was portraying it as "spiking."

Hogan went on to claim that the following week Dr. Morrow, the urologist, cultured the Jackson-Pratt drainage and found bacteria growing in it. In fact, it was urine from the bladder that he had cultured, not the Jackson-Pratt drain at all. I wondered if Hogan was just so poorly prepared that he really did not know that, or if he was trying to manipulate us into spending time arguing about things that really did not matter.

Hogan continued, "Around this time Dr. Cameron gets back from Europe and puts a note on the chart — 'Hey, no antibiotics are being given here'. That's in the chart right there on May 7th. That same day, antibiotics are finally started, but it's too late. On May 8th you will see the first note in the chart, 'pain in left leg'. And it goes downhill from there and she ends up losing her leg from a thrombophlebitis condition which is a clot. And she develops a condition called sepsis. Sepsis is nothing but infection getting into the blood stream. And when infection gets into the blood stream, it does lots of things; but one of the things it can do is form what's called emboli — little clots. They go around. They go through the heart, and the heart shoots them up to the brain and might shoot them to the lungs. In her case it shot one of them to the brain, and she had a stroke. And that's why she is partially paralyzed on her right side."

It seemed dreadfully wrong to me that our system allows

an attorney to mislead a jury with all manner of untruths and inaccuracies. Somehow it just didn't seem fair to me for us to have to try in a few short hours to educate fourteen jurors as to why what he was saying was not possible. It takes months to teach medical students the necessary anatomy and physiology for them to understand that clots which break loose from veins are filtered by the lungs and never "shoot up to the brain" unless the patient has an abnormal opening between the right and left sides of the heart, which Kathy did not have. How could the jury possibly be expected to decide where the truth lay?

"Through this combination of negligently severed ureter and substandard postoperative care, she now has an artificial leg and must write with her left hand. Because of these things, she has loss of employability, and she certainly has a difficult social life. She was twenty-six years old when this happened and she is now thirty. We are going to ask you for a verdict at the end. Our case will be based on what they put in that original medical chart before they were sued, before they saw lawyers, and when they were under an obligation, because of hospital regulations, to tell the truth. That's our evidence."

I could see that Tommy was right. If we tried too hard to convince the jury that Kathy never had sepsis and that all of her major problems related to her *Heparin* allergy, Hogan would try to convince them that we concocted that story as a result of the lawsuit and that the chart revealed the true story. In light of the gross distortions I had just heard, it seemed likely that he might succeed if we fought the sepsis theory too hard. Tommy's point was that sepsis is a recognized complication of pelvic exenteration, occurring even in the best of hands. Let Hogan claim that Kathy had it. If she did, it was managed appropriately.

The distortions had frustrated me. I wanted to jump up and say "That's not true. That's not right. That's a distortion." But I had to restrain myself. I had tried to prepare myself for the fact that everything Hogan said to the jury was not going to be medically accurate and that I would just have to sit there and take it, but it was more difficult than I had imagined. The pressure that I had felt before the trial increased enormously now that I was actually experiencing what it was going to be like. On the contrary, Hogan's opening statement had eased the pressure on Tommy and Charlie. They knew now that his case was going to be exactly what they thought it was going to be. They had properly prepared, and he was not going to surprise them with something they had not been anticipating.

Chapter 14

Monday Morning, August 26, 1985

> *Oratory is the power of beating down*
> *your adversary's arguments, and*
> *putting better in their place.*
> —Samuel Johnson

J ommy stood and walked across the room to the jury. His thick cropped, prematurely gray hair conferred a more distinguished appearance than most people achieve by their thirty-seventh birthday. As he began to speak, it was obvious that he was in his element — a modern day William Jennings Bryan who dearly loves to be in front of a jury pleading his client's cause. He began by telling the jury that a charge of negligence is the most serious civil charge that can be made against a doctor, and that his clients were not negligent, but acted with the highest level of skill.

"There is one fact that nobody will dispute," he said. "But for those two men sitting over there and the surgery they performed in January and April, Kathy Roberts would not be alive today. This is a case where two doctors undertook extensive, major, risky, complicated surgery and cured Kathy Roberts of a cancer that was killing her — that would have led to an excruciating, painful death long before now. Nobody can dispute that fact. Nobody will. Nobody dares."

It felt so much better having someone say something good about us. It had been a painful ordeal sitting there listening to Hogan lambaste us — an experience quite unlike any I had ever had before.

Tommy explained to the jury that all of our hearts went out to Kathy. We sympathized with her plight, and he didn't want anything we said to be mistaken for callousness. He continued with a rather detailed explanation of the events that had transpired with Kathy since her illness began, emphasizing the magnitude of her problems and the severity of her illness when Dr. Cameron was called into the operating room at her first operation in January, 1981.

"You see," he said, "after the January surgery she had a very high chance that she would die — even after that surgery. If there hadn't been the surgery she would have certainly died. The doctors will admit that. Even after surgery for cancer which has eaten through the colon most people don't make it. But when you have got a second cancer and you have to go back in again, the doctors will tell you chances are not good. They will tell you without it chances are zero. Those are the facts."

Tommy explained that Dr. Cameron had discussed the radical nature of the second operation with Kathy — all of the organs that would have to be removed, resulting in significant changes in her life style.

"Well the choice was between life or death, and she consented to it. And she placed no limits on him. She said 'Go in there and get all the cancer. I want it all out.' Now we heard the neat little thing where you just separate all these things out, and you don't worry about this, that, and the other. But you know, what's not always there is a mass of tumor, of cancer, of scar tissue from the previous cancer and infection. That's what existed in Kathy. Where the ureter was cut was where her cancer and the adhesions and the scar tissue from her already having cancer — from her already having surgery — had it bound down to the point that it couldn't be cut out without cutting the ureter. That's where it was cut.

"But, ladies and gentlemen, don't you be misled into thinking that cutting a ureter is an act always of carelessness or negligence like they contend. Dr. Lans, even his witness, will admit that when a ureter is bound down in cancer and adhesions, in some cases cutting it is unavoidable. Dr. Lans retired from surgery in 1979. He said the schedule was too tough. He didn't like the nights and weekends, so at the age of fifty-five he hung his surgical instruments up. By the time Kathy had to have an operation, he wasn't doing any operations on cancer patients in Chicago and he hasn't since then. It's been eight or ten years since he has done a procedure like this, and I want you to remember that when he gets on the stand and tells you how to do it.

"We will bring doctors from the University of Alabama in Birmingham, which is one of the leading cancer centers in this country today — does more of this surgery that we are

talking about probably than any institution in this country.
And these doctors will proudly tell you that Kathy Roberts
is alive today because she had the highest, the *highest*, level
of skill in her surgeons, and that they committed no malpractice.

"So Dr. Lans is wrong when he says cutting that ureter was
careless. They have to show this 'failure to use reasonable
care', and he is saying it was not reasonable to cut the ureter.
We are saying the evidence is overwhelming that that cut
ureter couldn't be avoided, and he will admit that it can't be
avoided many times.

"But see, that's not enough because they are asking you
here for damages because she lost her leg below the knee and
because she had a stroke which prevents her from writing
with her right hand. So he has got to say that cut ureter had
something to do with those two problems. And he says that
the urine was leaking and it caused sepsis. Sepsis is infection
— a generalized infection. He says that's what caused her to
lose the leg and have a stroke. Well, he has got some problems with that. You have some problems with that.

"She developed thrombophlebitis in the leg. That's all
throughout these records — well documented. She had
thromobophlebitis. Why do you get thrombophlebitis? It's
known to occur when somebody has cancer. It is a known
problem with cancer. Doctors will tell you if somebody has
thrombophlebitis that can't be explained otherwise, you
better look for cancer. And secondly it's known to occur
after major pelvic surgery. These doctors from Birmingham
will explain to you that it is a known problem with major
surgery like this, and they will say that it was treated appropriately. Unfortunately, it couldn't be cured, and she
had to have the leg amputated to save her life. The treatment
they gave her is *Heparin*. It is a blood thinner. It tries to

make the blood not clot. Oddly enough, sometimes it has the reverse effect — very rarely. There is very little known about it. That's what caused her to have the stroke — the treatment that they had to give for the thrombophlebitis.

"And I will tell you — this is very interesting. Dr. Lans says they should have called in a urologist — the specialist I referred to who treats the bladder and so forth. Well, Dr. Lans got involved in this case when some lawyers from Chicago represented the plaintiff. He has worked with those lawyers on ten cases or so. Now he said at that time they should have had a urologist, and the urologist should have treated this ureter and then maybe there wouldn't have been infection from the ureter. About two years after the suit was filed, the Chicago lawyers got around to taking the urologist's testimony — Dr. Tim Morrow. That was the last deposition they took in this case, because Dr. Morrow was asked in there, 'Dr. Morrow, did the cut ureter have anything to do with her losing a leg and having a stroke?'

"No. There is no relationship.'"

Tommy had an exaggerated, incredulous tone in his voice as he mocked Dr. Morrow in order to make his point to the jury.

"Dr. Morrow, was it repaired correctly?"

"'Yes.'"

"Dr. Morrow, did she suffer any permanent damage from the ureter having been cut?"

"'No. It healed fine. She is doing fine.'"

"He has followed her since the hospital," Tommy continued. "The very specialist who Dr. Lans says should have been involved says this cut ureter didn't have anything to do with this other. The cut ureter is on the right side. Her leg problem is on the left side. He says there is no relationship at all. That's the last we heard of the Chicago firm except for their motion to withdraw from the case.

"As I said earlier, anybody who has now heard what Kathy went through with her cancer and her surgery would, naturally, have feelings for her, and I don't deny those, nor do these doctors. But we are proud to say that Dr. Cameron and Dr. Snider will tell you that they acted with their best medical skill, judgment, and diligence. We are proud to tell you that these doctors will come down from the University of Alabama — Dr. Maddox and Dr. Orr — specialists, and tell you that without their efforts Kathy would have died from cancer or the complications that are known to go with it. And they will tell you, just as Dr. Morrow said, that cut ureter had nothing to do — had *nothing* to do with her leg or her stroke. And they will tell you that cutting a ureter in surgery like this is such an integral part of this surgery when the cancer is involved with the ureter — it is really such a minute part of this case — that they can't believe the criticism has been leveled.

"We will ask you at the end of the case to do something that hasn't been done — and that's to give these doctors thanks for saving a life. And the only way anything can do it now is with a verdict from you in favor of these defendants."

It all seemed so incongruent to me for these lawyers to be describing the same acts in such vastly different ways. Tommy and Charlie had never given us reason to believe that they viewed this case any differently from the way Dr. Cameron and I did. From our perspective, Kathy had received excellent care, and the lawsuit was grossly unjust. I assumed, and still do, that Tommy and Charlie were being honest with us in sharing that conviction. I wondered if Hogan really believed in the righteousness of his cause, or was he just pretending? Indeed, were all of them merely playing roles in a drama with no more conviction as to the veracity of their lines than actors in a play?

Chapter 15

Monday Afternoon, August 26, 1985

Face to face the truth comes out.

—Thomas Fuller

Seating of the jury and the attorneys' opening statements had taken the entire morning, so it was the afternoon session when Hogan began calling his witnesses. He began by calling the hospital administrator and asking him a few basic questions about hospital privileges and records. His second witness was Dr. Stuart May, the gynecologist who had initially operated upon Kathy in January, 1981. Apparently Hogan thought it was a significant point that Dr. May had treated Kathy for a urinary tract infection between her January and April operations and called him to testify in order to establish that fact. Hogan's implication was that Kathy had a urinary tract infection when she was operated upon in April and, therefore, was more likely to develop sepsis from a leakage of urine. Tommy took the wind out of that sail a little later by showing that she had a normal urinalysis just before the April surgery.

"Hogan's witness" made several statements that supported us: he saw no problems related to the cut ureter; most people who have cancer like Kathy's die from it; and Dr. Cameron had done an excellent job of caring for Kathy when he called him in. Hogan was not exactly off to a roaring start.

Hogan's next move was to call Dr. Cameron as an adverse witness against himself. My thought was that he was pretty hard up if he was going to have to use us as his witnesses, but apparently it is something plaintiffs' attorneys do frequently, the rationale being twofold. First, they hope to catch the defendant off guard — perhaps not completely prepared — make him nervous and rattle him early in front of the jury. Secondly, they want to give their own expert the advantage of knowing the defendant's testimony so that he can refute it when he testifies.

Hogan probably mistakenly asked Dr. Cameron to "describe for the jury the circumstances that you had when you came in and found her on the table and what you did and saw and so forth." A general question like that allowed Dr. Cameron to ramble in his homespun, folksy style about how "all this business was stuck together . . . and so forth." Anyone listening had to be impressed that he was most assuredly a "down to earth" person. He learned how to care for sick patients at Harvard University and the Mayo Clinic, but he learned how to talk in Faunsdale, Alabama.

Hogan began questioning Dr. Cameron about the location of the pelvic brim, which is the top part of the pelvis, and its relationship to the ureter and the location of the cancer mass that Dr. Cameron had biopsied. He spent a great deal of time on this issue and succeeded in engaging us in a debate that really had little relevance to the facts of the case. What he was trying to do was establish the fact that the ureter was cut some distance away from where the small mass of tumor was. What he did not understand, or perhaps did not want the jury to understand, is that when you have a recurrence after a colon cancer ruptures, you always have cancer cells spilled in multiple areas of the pelvis and there are potentially living and growing cancer cells throughout the scar tissue where the abscess was — not just in the one area where you can see and feel the cancer. If you are to have any hope of curing the patient in this situation, you must perform a wide, radical operation wherever the scar tissue is. The large abscess and the previous operation had filled Kathy's pelvis with scar tissue, literally up to the brim. So it really didn't matter whether the ureter was cut at the brim or down lower. We had to remove the scar tissue from all of the pelvis. This fact made Hogan's point moot.

Hogan projected a copy of the operative note onto a large screen so the jury could follow along as he read it, and asked Dr. Cameron to interpret it. Dr. Cameron again took advantage of this opportunity to drive home to the jury how difficult the operation was. Hogan was unable to keep Dr. Cameron responsive only to the questions without his elaborating on the things that needed to be said to the jury.

"You divide all the way around the pelvic brim, taking out the lymph glands and all the scar tissue that had formed from the previous abscesses and surgery and so forth that she had had in January," explained Dr. Cameron. "It was a real doggoned difficult procedure. We continued to do this, following the ureter down and so forth on both sides and, unfortunately, somewhere down in the pelvis we divided the right ureter in the midst of ——"

"Let me stop you there," interrupted Hogan. "I want to stop you there because I haven't asked you that yet, and I want to ask you that and I want to ask it in a certain way."

"Yes, sir," said Dr. Cameron.

"And you were the one that went out and talked to the family afterwards?" asked Hogan.

"Yes, sir."

"The only persons that were participating in that surgery were you and Dr. Snider. Is that right?" asked Hogan.

"That's true," agreed Dr. Cameron.

"Dr. Cameron, please look at this jury and tell them was it you or was it Dr. Snider that cut that ureter?"

Dr. Cameron looked dumbfounded. The absurdity of this implied accusation caught him off guard. However, he had been well coached and maintained his composure as he informed Hogan and the court that it was he who had cut the ureter.

Hogan asked, "You are not covering up for Dr. Snider are you?"

Tommy Keene jumped up. "Your honor, we object to that question. We are not covering up for anybody."

The judge overruled the objection and told Tommy to sit down.

Hogan continued. "Answer it. You can look at the jury and answer."

Dr. Cameron indignantly replied as he looked at the jury, "Of course not."

I was furious. Hogan was, I assumed, going to stoop to some rather low levels in order to plant seeds of doubt in the minds of the jurors. As I had been instructed, I sat still, trying not to reveal my anger and incredulity. It seemed wrong, though, to be trying to hide these strong feelings from the jury. It was so unnatural to try to cover up the anger I was feeling and to act unruffled. The things Hogan was saying did make me angry. I worried that the jury might interpret my lack of emotional response as meaning that the accusations did not bother me and were therefore legitimate. If Hogan continued with his innuendos, I knew it was going to be more difficult than I had thought to maintain my cool on the witness stand.

Hogan concluded this initial questioning of Dr. Cameron by asking him a series of hypothetical questions about cutting ureters. In the end Dr. Cameron acknowledged that if one dissected a ureter out completely throughout its length, knew exactly where it was, and then carelessly cut it anyway, that would probably be considered negligence.

The last witness Hogan called that first afternoon was Dr. Tim Morrow, the urologist that Lee DeWald had deposed shortly before he concluded that he didn't have a good enough case to pursue. I could not fathom why Hogan would call him as his witness when his testimony in the deposition had been so favorable toward us, but he did. When Dr. Morrow arrived at the courthouse to give his testimony, Hogan asked Dr. Cameron to step down. I breathed a sigh of relief. Defending himself against accusers of any kind was so alien to anything Dr. Cameron had ever done in his life, he had understandably been nervous about taking the stand. I knew now that Dr. Cameron was going to be just fine.

Much of Dr. Morrow's court testimony was just an explanation of the various drains and catheters that Kathy had, very little of which any of the jurors understood. As the questioning proceeded, it became obvious that Hogan was trying to establish that the urinary tract infection which Dr. May had diagnosed and treated in March had made it more likely that Kathy would develop sepsis from a cut ureter. He was asking his witness questions that he had not had an opportunity to ask him in deposition, so he really didn't know what his answers were going to be. It backfired on him. Dr. Morrow said that, in general, bladder infections are not serious problems and pose no health hazard to anyone. In his opinion, the minor urinary tract infection that Kathy had in March should have been cleared up within seven days — long before her April surgery — and that this was borne out by the normal urinalysis on admission to the hospital in April. He said that the reason she developed a urinary tract infection in April was that she had a catheter and that she had it because of the operation — not the cut ureter.

Hogan did manage to salvage one point to keep it from being a total loss. Although Dr. Morrow testified that when he came into the room everything was packed off so that he couldn't see for sure exactly where the ureter was cut, he thought it was somewhere around the pelvic brim.

During cross examination by Tommy Keene, Dr. Morrow dealt Hogan some substantial blows. Dr. Morrow said that he did not think the cut ureter had anything to do with the development of sepsis, and he didn't see how in the world it had any relationship to the development of phlebitis or a stroke. He supported another of our contentions by saying that he treats infections for a brief period of time, whenever possible, in order to prevent the development of resistant strains of bacteria. He told the jury that he had followed Kathy after she left the hospital and that her kidney and ureter were working fine. In short, she had suffered no permanent damage as a result of the cut ureter.

When the court session ended that day, Dr. Cameron and I and our attorneys went to their office to go over the events of the day and make plans for the following day. I was scheduled to be called to the stand the next morning as an adverse witness. Though I was a little apprehensive about it, I was also excited about the opportunity to match wits with Hogan. I knew I had nothing to hide and nothing to be ashamed of, and I was ready to tell my side of the story.

It was difficult sleeping that night. I tossed and turned for hours going over in my mind everything I wanted to say and how I wanted to say it. By 3:30 it was obvious that I was going to be unable to drift into the arms of Morpheus that night, so I took our puppy and went out to commune with nature.

Chapter 16

Tuesday Morning, August 27, 1985

> *Before beginning, prepare carefully*
> —Cicero

he few minutes of meditation in the rocking chair on our front patio was far more profitable to me than the hours of tossing and turning that had preceded it. There is nothing that is quite as tiring to me as trying unsuccessfully to fall asleep, and nothing that is quite as restful as the solitude of the early morning. The respite helped to calm my frayed nerves and get me in a better frame of mind to take the witness stand that morning. After Pam came out and offered to critique the terminology I was planning to use for the jury, we walked back inside the house, followed reluctantly by *Baby Doll,* who preferred to explore in the pre-dawn darkness.

I sat in the chair in front of my marine aquarium and watched the fish beginning to stir in response to the light in the room. There is something tranquilizing about watching fish gracefully and effortlessly glide through the water. No matter how stressed I feel, I can usually relax when I spend a little time communing with my fish. *Trigger* (a Picasso triggerfish) was still asleep, nestled head down in a niche among the branching limbs of a staghorn coral. I laughed to myself as I thought back to the first week we had *Trigger.* I had found him early one morning, upside down and motionless, and had been unable to arouse him by beating on the side of the tank. Convinced that he was moribund from polluted water, I spent the next hour changing the salt water in the tank, trying to rescue him from the jaws of death. I felt a sense of relief when he started swimming around and was obviously all right again. The following morning I found him in the same condition and changed the water again, thankful that I had awakened just in the nick of time. When it happened again the next morning, it finally dawned on me that he was not ill at all. It was just part of his unique personality to sleep upside down amidst the coral and to awaken whenever he pleased — not necessarily when I turned on the lights.

Beau (a Beau Gregory damselfish) peeked out from his cavern beneath the lava rock. He had excavated his own shelter beneath the rock by taking the small pieces of dolomite gravel one by one in his mouth and dropping them a distance away. Anytime the tank is cleaned or rearranged he can be observed over the next few days re-establishing his safe haven.

The Queen Angels were all up and looking for food. Often one reads that no more than one Queen Angel should be in a tank at a time because of their competitiveness and natural aggressiveness toward each other, but ours had done fine together. There is a definite "pecking order" among our queens with *Meg,* seven inches long, clearly the dominant fish in the tank. The smaller ones manage to do quite well though, darting in and out of crevices that she cannot negotiate. There was no way Pam and I were going to give up any of our queens in order to comply with advice to have only one in a tank. We had caught them all with a net and a "slurp gun" while scuba diving eighty feet deep on a natural "reef" several miles off the coast of Destin, Florida. As I sat there, I thought about Malcomb Patterson, captain of the dive boat *Triton,* from which we were diving when we caught the queens. Perhaps Malcomb had the right idea. He had a PhD in physiology and was on the faculty of Louisiana State University when he got tired of the hassle of academic life. He quit his job, moved to Destin, bought a boat, and began a charter service for deep sea fishing and diving. He developed his business into one of the classiest along the Gulf Coast and obviously enjoys it immensely.

Maybe I should move to Destin and get a boat, I thought.

Pam brought me a cup of coffee and sat down on the sofa.

"So, what are you going to tell the jury?" she asked.

"Well, one thing I want to do is get it across to them how everything in her pelvis was all socked in and hard to operate on," I said.

"What does 'socked in' mean?" asked Pam.

"You know — just all stuck together."

"Then say 'stuck together,'" she said. "I don't understand 'socked in' and neither will the jury, but we can understand 'stuck together.' I also think you need to come up with something that they can visualize in order to understand what it was like. Was it like glue had been poured in there?"

"Yeah. Superglue," I laughed.

"You need to illustrate it with something they can relate to," said Pam. "Would it be like trying to get gem clips out of a cup when they were glued together?"

"No. Not exactly."

"How is it different?"

"Well, the pelvis is bigger than a cup," I explained. "It's more like a bowl. And the organs we were removing were a lot larger than gem clips — more like fruit, I suppose."

"So it was like trying to get apples and oranges that were glued together out of a bowl?"

"Yeah. That's probably a pretty good analogy," I agreed.

"And what was the ureter like?" Pam asked.

"Well, I don't know — maybe like a string stuck in the glue. I think that is probably a pretty good illustration. It was like trying to get fruit out of a bowl without hurting the string when they were all glued together."

I went over this illustration in my mind and practiced it to Pam until I had it down. I then began my final review of all the notes that I had made in going over Kathy's chart and all of the depositions. Since my college days I have had a habit of overpreparing for everything in order to be absolutely certain that I would do well. Before taking my board exams in surgery I spent months and months studying every night and every weekend, reading and rereading the latest textbook of surgery from cover to cover. When it was time for the exam, I knew I was ready and I knew I would pass it without difficulty. I began to have that same feeling of confidence as I reviewed my notes that morning. I knew every word I had said in my deposition and was prepared to stand by every one. I knew what Dr. Lans had alleged in his deposition. I knew what Kathy's vital signs, physical findings, culture results, and other laboratory data had been each day. I knew what was in the doctors' progress notes and the nurses' notes each day.

I was absolutely convinced that Kathy had received excellent care throughout her hospitalization and had survived a catastrophic illness in large part because of that care, and I wanted the chance to tell my side of the story to the jury. I could feel my adrenalin flowing. I was beginning to eagerly anticipate testifying rather than dreading it. It was a feeling similar to what an athlete feels before a big game. I wanted the ball, and I was ready to run with it.

Chapter 17

> *Nothing gives one person so much*
> *advantage over another as to remain*
> *always cool and unruffled under all*
> *circumstances.*
> —Thomas Jefferson

*H*ogan called one of the nurses, Patsy Paschenko, who had participated in Kathy's April operation as his first witness of the second day. Why he did that, and what he hoped to accomplish by that move eludes me to this day. Everything she said supported our case, as it had in the deposition Mr. DeWald had taken long ago. I sensed that Hogan was already beginning to get frustrated when he finished with her and called me as an adverse witness.

I was self conscious as I walked to the witness stand, aware that the jurors were watching me. What were they thinking? Should I look at them and smile as I walked by — or would they consider that an insincere gesture designed to score points with them? If I did not smile at them would they consider me aloof and arrogant? I was beginning to resent having to think about such things — to be almost acting out a part in order to be sure to impress those who were keeping score and judging me. But it wasn't they whom I resented. It was the system. In the final analysis it seemed to me that we were not going to be judged so much by the facts in the case — no one was really going to completely understand them anyway. We were going to be judged more on how we impressed the jury, how our attorneys performed, and whether they swayed the jury better than Hogan.

Hogan began, as expected, by asking some basic questions about my educational background and training. He then turned the questioning to Kathy's case and my involvement in it. Tommy had told us to take every opportunity we had to hammer home the points we wanted to make. He had said, somewhat tongue in cheek, that George Wallace would make a good witness because he always ignores the questions that reporters ask and answers with whatever point he wants to make at the time — not at all unlike candidates in a presidential debate.

Hogan asked me about my recollections of the conversation Dr. Cameron and I had in the operating room when we discovered that the ureter had been severed. I took the opportunity to begin telling the jury how difficult the situation had been.

"I don't remember the details of the conversation," I began. "I remember that when the ureter was cut, it was in the middle of a lot of scar tissue where the area was very difficult to see. Everything in the pelvis was all stuck together. We couldn't tell what was ——"

"I wasn't asking you to get into that," Hogan finally interrupted. "What does it mean to dissect out the ureters?"

Again I was determined to communicate that this was not a straight forward, simple operation we had been doing.

"Well, in a case like this, when they are all bound down in a lot of scar tissue and everything is stuck together and you can't see what is going on, what you try to do is, with a knife, or scissors, or clamps or whatever, you try to get that ureter away from all of the scar tissue and the cancer and everything. You don't really have it dissected out until you've got it all the way down through all of this scar tissue and adhesions and everything."

I was being redundant, but I didn't want to leave any doubt about what the operative field had been like. Hogan asked me if Dr. Cameron was the one who cut the ureter and how it came to pass that I took care of her in his absence. He was trying to build a case that I was actually the one operating on Kathy — a "ghost surgeon" — and that I had cut the ureter. I was never sure whether he honestly suspected that or whether he just wanted the jury to suspect it.

He asked what was causing the drainage of urine to increase during the first week. Since he had told the jury in his opening statement that it was a sign of infection, I was delighted to have an opportunity to explain it.

"Well, where the ureter was sewn back together you always get drainage from those areas. That's why you put the drains there — to drain the urine to the outside. Frequently, when you are putting a ureter back together, there is a lot of tissue around it that sticks to the area and sort of plugs up the leaks. After a period of time, that stops the drainage. In Kathy, since we had taken everything — her rectum, and her uterus, and her vagina, her ovaries and tubes and all the lymph nodes and virtually everything else out of her pelvis — when we had finished, there was the ureter all by itself sort of flapping in the breeze with no tissue around it to plug up those holes or seal it. And so we knew that it was going to drain for a long period of time."

"Okay," Hogan said. "Can the drainage — the fact that it's increasing — be evidence of a problem going on?"

"No. Not as long as it's draining to the outside."

"Well, the fact that the drainage is increasing — doesn't that indicate any problem to you?"

"Not at all," I persisted. "That's common."

We then spent what to me seemed like an inordinate amount of time projecting all of the progress notes, nurses' notes, and order sheets from the chart onto a large screen in front of the jury and going over them day by day, reading every little bit of trivia in the chart for the entire week I was taking care of Kathy. I kept wondering what I had overlooked in the chart that Hogan was leading up to. I tried to scan a few lines ahead of him to anticipate what bombshell he was about to drop on the jury, but it never came. The notes supported the fact that she was doing quite well the entire week — sitting up, walking in the hall, smoking, watching television, visiting with friends, having one of her friends wash her hair, eating a regular diet — all of the things patients do when they are convalescing normally.

Hogan then turned his attention to the antibiotics that Dr. Cameron had ordered postoperatively. His whole contention was that I had stopped her antibiotics too soon and had not done any cultures. As a result of this, he contended, she had developed an infection which had somehow caused her phlebitis and her stroke.

"Why do you give antibiotics like that after the kind of surgery she had?" he asked.

"Well, you give antibiotics in this instance," I explained, "for what would be called prophylactic or preventive reasons. Any time you cut across the rectum or vagina you encounter bacteria, so you want to treat the patient for a very brief period of time with antibiotics to take care of any contamination at the time of surgery. As Dr. Morrow testified yesterday, we want to get the patient off of antibiotics just as soon as possible because there are problems associated with leaving the patient on antibiotics too long. So what we do just as soon as possible — if things are going well — is stop the antibiotics to prevent the development of resistant organisms, or organisms that no longer will respond to the antibiotic. As Dr. Morrow testified yesterday, if we get resistant organisms, they can invade the blood stream and kill the patient."

Hogan flashed an order sheet on the screen for the jury to read. "So you come along after two days and you countermand Dr. Cameron's order for three days of antibiotics?"

I was annoyed with Hogan's choice of the word "countermand," but I tried not to show it.

"No," I said. "I didn't countermand it. Dr. Cameron wanted the antibiotics stopped as soon as possible, which is why he wrote it for a very limited period of time. Kathy was doing so well at this point we were able to get her off of the antibiotics even sooner than he had anticipated, which is preferable. Now what we do is try to get patients off at twenty-four hours rather than forty-eight, if at all possible."

Hogan went through the notes from the remainder of that

first postoperative week and asked me about my consultation with Dr. Morrow on that Friday. He then looked at me
and shook his head as if in disgust and said, "And that's the
last you saw of the patient until after she was about to lose
her leg?"

The implication was that I had callously abandoned a
critically ill patient without so much as a thought for her
well-being. This allegation struck us and our lawyers as
being so absurd that we completely underestimated the impact that it had on the jury.

One of the major benefits of a group practice is that it
insures the surgeon adequate time off, knowing that his
patients will be managed with essentially the same level of
ability and skill as when he is around. Time off is essential
in order for a surgeon to remain fresh, capable of adroitly
handling the myriad of problems that arise on a daily
basis. Kathy had been an ordinary patient, convalescing
nicely from a major operation when I left for my weekend off. She was cared for the way we cared for all of
our patients. Dr. Ingalls, on call that weekend, saw her while
making rounds on Saturday and Sunday and was responsible
for her until Dr. Cameron returned on Monday. Since Dr.
Cameron had operated on her, he assumed her primary care
upon returning. Although I continued to follow her progress,
I did not make any more notes in the chart until my next
weekend on call, which was our usual custom.

Long before I joined the surgical group, my partners had
established a routine of having a group meeting every Monday morning to discuss the hospitalized patients and to offer
each other suggestions for their management. This tradition
helped to insure continuity of care and afforded the patients the benefit of multiple opinions. I had explained this
arrangement to the jury by saying, "Every Monday morning

we get together, all six of us now, and go over all of the patients and discuss the care of each, and communicate with each other and give each other ideas as to management." By "all six of us now" I meant that we had *six* partners now as opposed to the five we had when Kathy was in the hospital. I found out later that several of the jurors thought I meant that *now*, as a result of what we had learned from this case, all six of us get together and talk. They deduced that we must have had poor communication when Kathy was in the hospital. It never crossed our minds that the statement had been misunderstood. It is one of the little flaws in our system that the jurors really do not have an opportunity to ask questions in order to clear up misunderstandings like that.

Hogan continued asking about Dr. Morrow's involvement in the case, trying to establish that we had asked him to see Kathy *only* about her catheter and not to help with any other aspect of her care. Tommy had somehow anticipated that he would do that and, for reasons which eluded me, wanted me to be sure to communicate to the jury that I knew Dr. Morrow would take over the care of her urinary problems at that time. To this day I am not sure why that point seemed so important to both sides. Again, I found myself caught in an alien game, avoiding direct answers to questions which seemed completely irrelevant to me.

"Well," said Hogan. "You asked Dr. Morrow a fairly specific question, as he testified yesterday, about the catheter, didn't you?"

"Well, I knew that Dr. Morrow would come in and, at that point, take over the care of the urinary system, as he did," I responded. "I knew that he would come in and feel free to write any order that he wanted to, to order any test that he wanted to. And the very first time he saw the patient he ordered an IVP, an intravenous pyelogram. Several days later he felt fre ——''

"Just answer my question, please!" Hogan snapped, his frustration giving way to anger. "You can answer that question ——"

Tommy and Charlie simultaneously jumped from their seats.

"He is answering the question," Tommy said to the judge.

"If it please the court," said Charlie, "the lawyer wants to cut him off."

Judge Price held his hand up and shook it back and forth to calm both sides down. "Wait a minute. Do you object?" he asked Charlie.

"Yes, sir," responded Charlie. "We object to the lawyer cutting off the witness."

"All right," said the judge, turning to Hogan. "Don't cut the witness off. Mr. Hogan, you ask the questions. Dr. Snider, you wait until the question is asked fully before you try to answer. Mr. Hogan, you wait until he finishes answering the question before you ask another question. Respond specifically to the question," he added, looking at me.

Thus far I was feeling good about the way things were going. I was feeling more comfortable on the witness stand and was able to maintain my composure. Hogan, on the other hand, seemed to be rattled and his composure appeared to be slipping.

"Had Dr. Ingalls had any involvement in this case before this day?" he asked, turning his attention to the weekend when Dr. Ingalls had been on call.

"He had not operated in the case," I said, "but I reviewed in detail with him, before leaving for the weekend, everything that had transpired up to that point, as I do in all the patients before I leave for the weekend."

"Would any review that you may have had with him have included such detail that he would have had knowledge of the kind of surgery that was involved and the fact that antibiotics were cut off on this patient?" he asked.

"Absolutely," I answered.

"Now let me ask you something," Hogan continued. "There are no notes from anyone in your service on May 4th or May 5th. Were you relying on Dr. Morrow to take over your patient on those two days?"

Dr. Cameron had returned and was taking care of Kathy on those days but had failed to record anything in the progress notes. When I had joined the group in 1976, it was not at all unusual for my partners to go for several days at a time without writing a progress note. They took excellent care of the patients but just didn't always document it. By 1981 everyone in the group almost always wrote daily notes but occasionally skipped a day or so. Unfortunately, there were two days out of the entire two month hospitalization that no one from our group wrote a note. I pointed out that the nurses' notes reflected that Dr. Cameron had seen her on rounds during that time but that he had just not written a note. Hogan was trying to convince the jury that we had "abandoned" her and left poor Dr. Morrow to take up the slack. He was doing a better job of that than I gave him credit for at the time.

Hogan flashed a copy of the progress notes on the screen and showed the jury a note Dr. Cameron had written later in the week which read "Temperature to 101.6. Not on antibiotics."

"Dr. Snider, how do you interpret this 'Not on antibiotics.' Is this your report card?" he said, with a condescending sneer.

"Sir?" I asked, momentarily taken aback.

"Is the reason that the patient was at a temperature of 101.6 because she was not on antibiotics?" he asked.

"Absolutely not," I countered, regaining my composure. "That is a note by Dr. Cameron that for the first time her temperature has gone up to 101.6 and he is making a note to himself and others that she is not on antibiotics. It is by no means implying that she should be. As a matter of fact, he didn't start her on antibiotics. She is his patient. He is primarily responsible. If he felt like she should have been on antibiotics, he would have written an order at that time."

"Well, don't you know that Dr. Morrow did order antibiotics that day?" asked Hogan.

"After he saw the result of the urine culture and the temperature and felt like she might have, perhaps, a minor urinary tract infection," I explained. "He testified that he treated a minor urinary tract infection."

By the time Dr. Morrow came by that day, the results of a urine culture had come back showing a urinary tract infection, and he had appropriately begun antibiotics because of the combination of the increasing fever and the culture results.

"Well, is that a good idea to treat with antibiotics on May 7th?" Hogan asked.

"I think it was reasonable, yes," I responded.

"Was it a good idea to culture this patient as Dr. Morrow did on May 5th?" he continued.

"Well somewhere along in there, after a catheter has been in for a week, ten days, something like that, you are going to have organisms growing there. You don't treat that, as Dr. Morrow testified yesterday, just because organisms are growing there. All that means is it is colonized. It does not mean infected."

Hogan was allowing me to ramble so I turned to the jury and continued to explain the concept.

"I think this is a very important point. We don't treat colonization because if we did, everybody in this room would be on antibiotics right now. We all have bacteria growing all over us — in our mouths, in our intestines, in the rectum, in the vagina. Some of us have organisms growing in our gallbladders. They're all over our skin and our hair. That's colonization and that's what Dr. Morrow was referring to yesterday when he said if you did a urine culture and grew bacteria, that would be colonized, but that he wouldn't necessarily treat that. The reason he is treating it here is because there is a combination of that colonization plus, for the first time, a fever to 101.6. He put those two together and felt like, perhaps, this was a minor urinary tract infection and needed treating. And I agree with that."

"You are saying this was the first time there was a temperature?" Hogan asked.

"No," I said. "The first time there was a temperature to 101.6."

"The next note there," said Hogan, turning back toward the screen. "'Pain in the left leg and lower thigh.' And that's where it all starts, isn't it?"

"I am not sure what you mean by 'that's where it all starts,'" I said.

"Isn't that the first day that we have some evidence that now she has thrombophlebitis?" asked Hogan.

"No," I said. "I think we had evidence back on the 7th, certainly when she had a temperature of 101.6. That may well have been from thrombophlebitis that she had that temperature. No one can say for sure whether it was the thrombophlebitis causing that temperature, the minor urinary tract infection, or a combination of the two."

"I want to just summarize some things and I'm through," said Hogan. "First of all, you were there during the surgery. You saw the ureter cut. Is that correct?"

"That's correct."

"You were given the primary responsibility to look after this patient while Dr. Cameron was away. Is that correct?"

"That's correct."

"You came in and issued the order that cut off the antibiotics on April 25th. Is that true?"

"That's correct."

"At no time during the time you were watching this patient, all the time up to the time of May 1st when you left the chart, you never ordered any type of culture on this patient?"

"No sir. That's not true," I responded.

Hogan had his rhythm going, and he was fully expecting me to agree that I had ordered no cultures. When I didn't agree, he wheeled and looked at me in astonishment.

"What culture did you order?" he asked, the self-assured smirk gone from his face.

"Well," I explained, "You don't culture things like urine or drain sites or things like that because you know they're going to be colonized — or, at least, I don't. And I was trained ——"

Hogan was furious.

"Your honor, I would ask the court to direct the witness to answer the question," Hogan shouted. "My question was did he order any cultures?"

"Yes," I replied.

Hogan, still steaming, asked, "What was the culture that you ordered?"

"I cultured the tip of the subclavian catheter which was in her blood stream," I explained. "The one exception to treating patients just because the bacteria are there is if the bacteria are in the blood stream. So, on April 30th, I did a routine surveillance type culture just to be sure she didn't have any bacteria growing in her blood stream. There was no reason whatsoever to suspect that there might be, but I exercised what I considered to be good judgment by sending that catheter down to culture it just to be certain. If it had grown bacteria, I would have treated that. There was no other culture that I could have ordered that — if it had shown bacteria — I would have treated. It would have just shown colonization, and treatment of that would have only been harmful and not helpful."

Hogan, apparently reeling, had, I assumed, hoped to have a strong finish with me by having me tell the jury that I had ordered no cultures. In the limited time that he had had to prepare for the case, he had, I believe, overlooked some important points. In my judgment, he had also erred by asking Dr. Morrow a question about single blood cultures the day before, because it tipped me off to be particularly prepared on that point — and I was.

Hogan tried to salvage things by making that point now.

"Was there more than one blood culture ever ordered on this patient the whole time she was in the hospital?" he asked.

"Yes, sir. She had three," I answered.

Hogan looked dumbfounded. He swallowed hard and picked up the hospital record.

"Well now, will you find that for us in the record?" he stammered.

"The catheter tip was sent down on April 30th," I said. "The blood was again cultured on May 15th, and then a catheter tip was again cultured on June 16th."

"Is that a blood culture?" he asked.

"Well, sure," I said. "A subclavian catheter is right in the blood stream and when you have bacteria in the blood, they tend to collect on foreign bodies that are in the blood stream. The catheter is in the blood stream so that's a good way of checking to see whether there are any bacteria in the blood."

"Do you take, as part of this culture, a part of the patient's blood and culture it?" Hogan asked.

"You culture the tip of the catheter that has the blood in it," I responded.

Hogan handed me a sheet from the chart that had the blood culture result from May 15 listed on it. The catheter tip cultures were on separate sheets which he did not show me.

"How many blood cultures does it show were given to Kathy Roberts the entire time she was in the hospital?" he asked.

"On this sheet," I responded, "it shows one blood culture on May 15; but there were really other cultures with catheters from the blood, with blood on them, which is a means of culturing blood."

"In any event," said Hogan, "to finish the summarization, you never cultured either the Jackson-Pratt drainage, or the Penrose drainage, or the urine drainage from the Foley catheter. True?"

"That's correct," I said, "and the reason I did not culture those, once again, is because it would not have changed her treatment one bit regardless of what bacteria was growing in it."

"You are saying you wouldn't have given any antibiotics even if you had seen a positive result?" asked Hogan.

"Absolutely not," I said.

Hogan was really ineffective by this point. He was giving me such nice opportunities to explain things to the jury, there wouldn't be much left for Tommy to ask me if he persisted much longer.

"As a matter of fact," I continued, "it would have been the wrong thing to do. And she is probably alive today because we judiciously used antibiotics only when we needed them and did not have her on antibiotics when she didn't need them."

Hogan was still allowing me to ramble.

"If you put people on antibiotics, like Dr. Morrow testified yesterday, and you leave them on them for a period of time, they are going to develop resistance to those antibiotics as Kathy Roberts did. The Enterobacter that we have already referred to was originally resistant only to *Ampicillin* and *Cephalothin*. She was on *Geocillin* for one week, and before she left the hospital, that same organism was resistant to *Geocillin*."

"What are the signs of infection?" Hogan asked, his voice conveying, to me, the hostility that I saw in him.

"Well," I said, "I believe yesterday you told the jury that the signs of infection that I ignored were twofold. One was drainage of urine. That is categorically absolutely not ——"

"Will you answer the question," shouted Hogan, his face red with anger. "Tell me what the signs of infection are!"

"Okay," I began. "The signs of infection are not drainage of urine ——"

"Tell me what the signs of infection are," screamed Hogan, louder than before.

"One sign of infection," I continued, "would be a spiking, high fever, which Kathy Roberts did not have."

"What is another sign of infection?" snapped Hogan.

"Well, a patient who is septic acts sick. She is not up out of bed, walking to the nurses' station, eating a regular diet, washing her hair, watching television, sitting up in bed ——"

"All right," interrupted Hogan, "What's another sign of infection?"

I explained that pain could be a sign of infection in cases of boils and so forth, but not in this case, and that an elevated white blood count could be a sign of infection. In response to his question, I told Hogan I didn't order a white count on Kathy because it would not have altered the way I treated her. Since she was doing well clinically, I would have considered it wrong to treat an elevated white count.

Hogan apparently could see that he was not getting anywhere, so he told the judge he had no further questions. I breathed a sigh of relief as Judge Price told the jury to take a ten minute recess. The worst part was over. Although I could not read all of the jurors, there was one smiling face in the middle of the back row that I felt certain was with us. I later told Tommy and Charlie that I thought her vote was in the bag.

Chapter 18

Tuesday Morning, August 27, 1985

*He who has the truth at his heart
need never fear the want of
persuasion on his tongue.*
—John Ruskin

*I*t would not be completely accurate to say that I had enjoyed the mental joust with Hogan, but it was better than having Hogan addressing the jury alone, with no one to expose his inaccuracies. It was even better having Tommy question me. I knew basically the things he was going to be asking me and knew that there was little chance that I would end up saying anything wrong. He began with questions which led me into telling the jury that I had been in several honor societies at the University of Alabama, one of which was Phi Beta Kappa, and that I had been accepted to the Medical College of Alabama during my third year of college with a perfect grade point average. He elicited that I had graduated from medical school ranked second in a class of eighty students, having been inducted into Alpha Omega Alpha medical honor society during my third year. I told about my surgical internship at Johns Hopkins Hospital and my residency at the University of Alabama Hospital in Birmingham, a total of nine years of training after college. He asked about Dr. John Kirklin, who had been the Chief of Surgery during my residency — my teacher. He made a point of asking if it was the same Dr. Kirklin who was formerly at the Mayo Clinic, knowing fully well that it was. We covered the medical societies that I was a member of, articles that I had published in the medical literature, and the fact that I was certified as a specialist by the American Board of Surgery.

Tommy got me to tell how it happened that I had joined the group in Montgomery — that Dr. Kirklin had told me, when I was still a resident, about Dr. Cameron, his classmate at Harvard and the Mayo Clinic, whom he held in such high esteem. He told me that I would be fortunate, indeed, if I could get a job in Dr. Cameron's group.

I had forgotten to look at the jury and talk to them during the first few minutes. Tommy walked over to the far side of the jury box as a gentle reminder that I was supposed to be talking to them and not him. He turned his line of questioning to Kathy's case and made certain the jury understood how serious her problem had been. I reiterated the point that an operation like hers had to be extensive and radical in order to try to remove all of

the cancer cells which were mixed with scar tissue throughout the pelvis. Tommy made sure the jury knew what Kathy
had been up against.

"Okay," said Tommy, "as of January, with the colon
cancer that Kathy had, without surgery what would have
happened to Kathy?"

"She would have died."

"Now, in dealing with cancers of this sort, we hear the
term 'mortality rate'. Is that a familiar term to you?"

"Very much so," I said.

"You are saying that without surgery, mortality is one
hundred percent?"

"That's correct," I agreed.

"That's certain," Tommy added for emphasis. "Even
with the type of surgery that you have described for us, are
there recognized mortality rates with this kind of cancer that
Kathy suffered from?"

"Absolutely."

"What kind of mortality rates are reported and experienced by doctors doing these types of operations?"

"Oh, the chance that a patient would die from the operation would be in the neighborhood of ten or fifteen percent,
or higher."

"How about the chances that even after the operation the
patient does not survive as long as three or four years?"

"That chance is in the neighborhood of ninety percent.
Of patients who have a recurrent carcinoma from the colon
that has perforated and eaten through and is growing again
in the pelvis, about one in ten you can cure with a radical
operation."

Tommy asked about the complications of this radical operation, eliciting that thrombophlebitis can occur in people
walking the streets, but that it is much more common after

major operations, totally unrelated to whether or not the patient has an infection. We discussed that the gangrene that people occasionally get in their legs from phlebitis is caused by clots blocking all of the veins so that blood cannot get out of the leg. As the leg swells, there is no place for fresh blood to go, so the tissues die from lack of oxygen, again completely unrelated to infection. Tommy then gave me a chance to illustrate what it was like to be operating in Kathy's pelvis.

"I will ask you to now define for us what is meant by this term 'everything in the pelvis was tightly bound down,'" he said. "Could you please try to give me and everybody here who hasn't operated and been inside of a pelvis the benefit of the best explanation of what that presents to the surgeon?"

"Obviously, it's difficult to describe something to someone who has never seen it. I think Ms. Paschenko's description of it this morning was 'sort of like concrete'. I think that is a reasonable description. Everything in the pelvis in Kathy was stuck together," I said, remembering Pam's admonition to say "stuck together" instead of "socked in." "It was distorted so that we couldn't tell the difference in the rectum, uterus, vagina, ovaries or ureters. It was just all balled together in one great big mass of scar tissue that filled the pelvis, literally up to the brim. Perhaps an illustration would be, if I took a bowl of fruit and considered the fruit the different organs that were in there — the apples and oranges would be the colon and the uterus and that sort of thing — and I put several strings down into that bowl of fruit, and those strings represented ureters or arteries or nerves or things like that, and asked you to take out those organs in there without cutting the strings. You can reach in and very easily take out the apples and oranges and fruit and leave the strings behind. But if I then came along and took a big bottle of superglue and poured it in and filled that bowl literally up to the brim and then I told you to go in and take out the apples and oranges but don't cut any of the strings — and you can't take that superglue out of the bowl. You are going to have to work down in the bowl, just like we had to work down in the bony confines of Kathy's pelvis, and take those apples and oranges out from that superglue without cutting a string — I think that's about as close as I can come to describing what we were up against."

"Can you visualize and dissect out the ureters at one point and not in another in some cases?" Tommy asked.

"Yes."

"Is this the way it is in all cases?"

"Not in all cases," I responded. "When there has been no previous operation or infection and there is no scar tissue, you can dissect them out relatively easily all of the way."

"So does it depend on the prior disease the patient has had and the prior operations the patient has had to undergo?"

"Yes."

"Now in this case," Tommy asked, was a ureter visualized up in the abdominal area?"

"Yes."

"And then as you got into this mass you've described as being like concrete, were you or Dr. Cameron able to see it before it was cut?"

"No."

"In fact, after it was cut, I believe you said 'I *think* this is a tube,'" Tommy exclaimed.

"I think Ms. Paschenko said that I thought it was a tube, implying that I couldn't tell for sure."

"Well, why would that be?"

"Well, when it's in the midst of all of this scar tissue —

when things are distorted and we can't tell the difference between the rectum and the ureter — when you are looking at
it, it's very difficult to tell what it is."

"Do you cut tissue in addition to just the rectum, vagina,
uterus and ovaries?"

"Sure."

"Why do you have to cut out all of that surrounding tissue in those organs?"

"Dr. Cameron knew that there was one area of cancer
there that he had biopsied, but almost for sure, there were
other areas of cancer throughout all of that scar tissue.
When the colon ruptures and carries cells out, it carries a
lot of different cells and they implant in different areas. The
biggest group of those cells is the one that grows to the point
where you can feel it first and see it and biopsy it. But, almost for sure, there are other cells there that are growing and
that just haven't gotten big enough to where you can feel
them and see them. So a cardinal principle of cancer surgery
is to get wide around all of that area — take it all out — so
that you get it and get all of the cancer cells out. If we had
missed them that time and they had come back, there would
be no way of curing Kathy and she would have died from the
cancer."

Tommy then shifted to the postoperative period when I
was caring for Kathy and asked what I considered to be a
high fever.

"Well," I began, "you have to take it in context. The first
day after a major operation like Kathy had, when you have
a lot of tissue dissection and bleeding in the tissues, and when
she has been asleep for a long period of time and has little
areas of collapse of the lungs called atelectasis, everyone
has a fever. And hers was 101.0 that first day. That is
really fairly low for the first postoperative day. It would

not be unusual at all for it to be higher than that. So, taken in context, 101.0 is certainly not a high fever for the first day postoperatively."

"As you go on through the postoperative days, what temperature causes you to think of infection?"

"Frequently, 101.5 is used as a cut off point. Something less than that postoperatively for a period of time is not of any concern."

We again went over the antibiotics, and why it is important to get the patient off of them as soon as possible to prevent the development of resistant organisms. We reiterated that cultures would not have changed things because we would not have treated the bacteria that would grow. Tommy asked about Dr. Morrow's involvement in the case and whether we had placed any restrictions on his freedom to write orders, pointing out that Dr. Morrow had ordered a test on the very first day he saw her.

"And then it was another four days before he decided that a culture even needed to be taken, wasn't it?" he asked.

"That's correct."

"And then it was six or seven days before he decided to treat what he called her urinary tract infection with an antibiotic?"

"That's correct."

"You didn't at any time limit his ability to order those tests or give those medicines, did you?"

"Not at all."

"Dr. Snider, based on your surgical training and experience, in your opinion, could Dr. Cameron have avoided cutting the ureter and still been able to remove what he had to remove to cure the cancer?"

"No."

"In your opinion, did the fact that the ureter was cut in

the process of removing this cancer and scar tissue indicate that he was careless or negligent or failed to exercise reasonable care in any way?"

"Certainly not."

"And I will ask you whether, in your opinion, based on your care and treatment of that patient in the hospital, that the cut ureter had anything to do with Kathy Roberts' developing thromophlebitis?"

"Nothing whatsoever."

"Do you agree with Dr. Morrow, who testified yesterday, that he saw no relationship at all?"

"I agree completely with Dr. Morrow on that."

"Did that cut ureter have anything to do with her developing gangrene in that left leg and having to have it amputated?"

"Nothing at all."

"Was that something which occurred as a result of the cancer and the surgery she had for it?"

"Yes."

"And were attempts made to prevent that thrombophlebitis and to treat it?"

"Sure."

"And were those treatments standard and appropriate to try to counteract that blood clotting?"

"Yes."

"Can a doctor always counteract and cure thrombophlebitis after surgery like Kathy had?"

"By no means."

It was, of course, much easier for Tommy to develop a rhythm since I was answering all of his questions affirmatively. I was certain that things would not go as smoothly in the afternoon session when he was cross examining Dr. Lans.

Chapter 19

Tuesday Afternoon, August 27, 1985

> *The Truth may stretch but will*
> *never break.*
> —Cervantes

Hyman Lans is unprepossessing in appearance; – his voice unanimated. I was surprised when he told the jury that he had graduated from Princeton and had been in Alpha Omega Alpha and was ranked second in his class in medical school at

the University of Illinois College of Medicine. Whatever
else he may have been, he was not dumb.

After the initial general questions, Hogan put a copy of the
discharge summary and consultation sheets on the screen
and read them to the jury, with Dr. Lans explaining the
medical terminology and his interpretation of the events
that had transpired. Hogan then asked Dr. Lans to draw a
diagram of the anatomy and show the jury where he understood the ureter had been cut. Dr. Lans indicated that he
thought the ureter was cut at the pelvic brim, far away from
where the cancer had been biopsied in the recto-vaginal sep-
tum. According to his neat little drawing, the cancer was
in one isolated little spot and the ureter was cut far away.
He, of course, did not include the pelvis full of scar tissue
in his drawing, nor did he indicate that the scar tissue went
right up to the pelvic brim where he said the ureter had been
cut. The point they were making was really moot, but later
they succeeded in engaging us in a debate about it anyway.

Dr. Lans said we should have been investigating the "spiking fever" that Kathy had in the postoperative period. It
is easy to sit in the comfort and security of one's office,
armed with the luxury of knowing the outcome of a case,
and speculate on all kinds of things that could have been
done differently. Regardless of how extensively we in-
vestigated her postoperative fever, her treatment would
have remained the same. However, if an extensive evaluation was done for every little fever in all patients having
the smooth recovery Kathy was having early in her course,
the cost of medical care would increase enormously — with
very little benefit to the patient. As Dr. Lans was speaking,
I thought about the increasing necessity to practice medicine defensively — to order tests that aren't necessary in

providing excellent care of the patient, but that you may later wish you had ordered to defend yourself in court. In 1983, the American Medical Association Committee on Professional Liability estimated that between fifteen and forty billion dollars are spent annually in the United States for defensive medicine. I knew that I would be contributing a much larger share to that figure in the future.

Dr. Lans said that it was his opinion that the ureter was cut in an area away from the cancer and adhesions, that it was avoidable, and was, therefore, substandard surgical care of the patient. He said that it was below the minimum standard of care for me not to culture the drainage during that first week and that I should have continued her antibiotics.

Plaintiffs' lawyers say that doctors take charges of negligence too personally — that we should understand it is not really personal and allow it to roll off our backs — develop thicker skin. But it is deeply and intensely personal and penetrates to the very depths of my being when someone says I am negligent. I would not want someone treating me who thought it no big deal to be accused of negligence, and I suspect the plaintiffs' attorneys feel the same way.

Hogan asked Dr. Lans, "Do you have a judgment as to whether these deviations from the minimal standard of care that you have just described, with a reasonable degree of medical probability, caused or led to her loss of her leg and her stroke?"

I was most interested in hearing this response. Hogan had told the jury in his opening statement that the testimony would show that her "sepsis" caused her to shoot a clot up to her brain and cause the stroke. If Dr. Lans supported that contention, he would have been clearly perjuring himself.

Dr. Lans' answer was rambling, the bottom line of which was that the cut ureter caused sepsis, which caused thrombophlebitis, which caused gangrene of the leg. He did not explain how the presumed sepsis (which she did not have) would have been a more likely cause of phlebitis than the known common causes of surgery, cancer and obesity. He also did not explain why, if his theory were valid, the phlebitis developed on the opposite side of the body from where the ureter was cut. More importantly, he failed to mention anything about her stroke, and Hogan never asked him about it again. No testimony at any time supported Hogan's allegation to the jury that an infection in her blood stream shot a clot up to her brain and caused her stroke. It seemed to me that either Hogan had been deliberately misleading the jury in his opening statement with allegations he could not support, or *he* was negligent in forgetting to get his witness to support the contention. It did not seem right to me that he could commit either of those grievous errors and not be held accountable.

As Hogan finished his questioning, I found myself hoping that the jury shared my opinion of his case — that it was really very thin and very transparent. This was the bulk of his case — this one hired witness. He would, of course, put Kathy and a few others on the stand later to try to sway the jury through sympathy; but after Dr. Lans finished, there would be no more testimony that her care had been anything less than excellent. I wondered to myself, if we stopped right there and sent the case to the jury, how they would rule.

Tommy approached the witness stand and began his cross examination. It was evident that he relished the opportunity to pick away at Dr. Lans' testimony. By nature Tommy is fiercely competitive and always has been. To him a courtroom battle is like a medieval joust, conferring glory on the victor and unspeakable dishonor on the vanquished.

He began questioning Dr. Lans deliberately and courteous-
ly; but I knew that, beneath Tommy's docile veneer, a serpent
was coiled, poised to strike at inaccuracies and distortions.
Dr. Lans acknowledged that he was now semi-retired because
the life of a surgeon was too hectic for him. In fact, he had
not done a case like the one in question for almost ten years.
In all of his twenty-five years of practice, he had done only
about fifteen pelvic exenterations. He worked only three
days a week now and limited his surgery to minor outpatient
work.

Dr. Lans agreed with Tommy that Kathy's operation had
been extensive, and with such extensive procedures there was
a substantial risk involved — even a risk of dying — but that
without the operation she faced certain death. He acknowledged that even if the surgeon and the whole team do an
excellent job, a patient may experience complications and
die — and that it would be no one's fault. He said that in
pelvic exenterations there are times when the ureter has to
be intentionally divided, and the surgeon may not know until
he gets into the abdomen whether or not that will be necessary. The questioning then turned to unintentional division
of the ureter.

"You acknowledge," Tommy asked, "that there may be
cases where the ureter is bound down to the extent that it
is unavoidable for the surgeon to cut it?"

"That's true."

"All right. You also acknowledge that the ureter may be
. . . how long do you think it is?"

"Twelve inches," said Dr. Lans.

"All right. There may be cases where seven or eight of
those twelve inches are clearly visible, but the last three or
four may be bound down in a mass?"

"The last three or four may be bound down," agreed Dr.
Lans.

"All right. And in that instance, it may be unavoidable for the surgeon to cut the ureter?" asked Tommy.

"In that instance, yes."

"So you certainly acknowledge that the circumstance can exist in general," continued Tommy.

"It can exist in a particular case," agreed Dr. Lans.

"You are just saying that, based on the way that you read this case, you don't think that is the way that it happened here?"

"From the operative report and the testimony I've heard here, I don't believe that was the case," asserted Dr. Lans.

"Well, of course," said Tommy, "you have heard the testimony from Dr. Cameron and Dr. Snider that it was bound down."

"And from Dr. Morrow that it was higher up," added Dr. Lans.

"Well, Dr. Morrow was not there when it was cut, was he?" asked Tommy.

"He was there when they were repairing it," said Dr. Lans.

"Yes," said Tommy. "You heard him say 'when I came in, they had already dissected on down and freed it up for the repair?'"

"I heard him state," said Dr. Lans, "when he was directly asked where it was cut, he said 'at the pelvic brim.'"

"Well, let me ask you. What you are necessarily doing is rejecting Dr. Cameron's and Dr. Snider's testimony, isn't it?"

"No," said Dr. Lans. "I am going by Dr. Cameron's operative report, which is all I have to go by."

"That's all you have to go by?" questioned Tommy.

"As far as their part of the record is concerned," said Dr. Lans.

"But you are willing to take Dr. Morrow's testimony?"

"Which I heard here," nodded Dr. Lans.

"Okay," said Tommy. "Didn't you also hear him say that, in his opinion, the cut ureter didn't have any relationship to her leg or her stroke?"

"That's his opinion as to that relationship," agreed Dr. Lans, "but when he was asked if it was cut at the brim of the pelvis, he said 'yes.'"

"I understand," said Tommy. "You are accepting what he said about the brim of the pelvis, but you disagree with what he said about whether the ureter had anything to do with the leg or the stroke, aren't you?"

"One I believe is a fact, which is the location of the cut," said Dr. Lans. "The other is his opinion, based on his judgment. I differentiate between the two."

"Well, aren't you telling this court you don't agree with Dr. Morrow's opinion?" asked Tommy.

"In that portion, I do not agree with him," responded Dr. Lans.

"Well," said Tommy, "That was a pretty basic portion wasn't it — whether the cut ureter had anything to do with the leg or the stroke?"

"No. I believe there could be a difference of opinion there based on the record."

"Okay," said Tommy, "but you want to accept what he said about the location?"

"Yes."

Dr. Lans and Tommy debated the semantics of Dr. Cameron's operative note and whether the ureter had been cut in an area where it was bound down in scar tissue. Dr. Lans acknowledged that a ureter can be hidden in one location and not in the other, but that in this case he thought it had been cut in its midportion, away from the scar tissue. Tommy reminded Dr. Lans that in his deposition he had testified

that the ureter had been cut in its lower third, a fact that
Dr. Lans had apparently forgotten. Dr. Lans did some fancy
double talking and basically ended up saying that, although
the pelvic brim is right at the midportion of the ureter, he
did not think it inconsistent that the ureter could be cut in
its lower third at that location — a statement which made no
sense at all to me. I hoped that the jury would realize that
he had changed his testimony to fit the case Hogan was trying to build, but I was not at all certain they were following the testimony that closely.

Tommy showed Dr. Lans a copy of the pathology report
of the specimen which had been removed from Kathy, and
put an enlarged copy of the document where the jury could
read it also. The point that he was making was that the pathologist, even after having the specimen out on the dissecting table, had a difficult time identifying the organs. His
description was that "this entire area is a mass of adhesions
and hemorrhage, and a discrete mass lesion is not identifiable."

Tommy then turned the line of questioning to infection which may occur after pelvic exenterations. Dr. Lans
acknowledged that an infection may occur, regardless of
whether the ureter has been cut, because the rectum and
vagina must be cut. He agreed that the infection may lead
to sepsis, and the patient might die despite proper treatment, and that it would not necessarily be the fault of the
surgeon. He said that the consultants on the case had mentioned sepsis only as a possibility, and not as an established
fact.

Dr. Lans agreed with Tommy that fever can occur unrelated to infection for the first few days after an operation
and that one of the causes for fever could be thrombophlebitis regardless of whether or not she had an infection.

Tommy again made the point that her ureter was cut on the right side and her phlebitis developed on the left side.

Dr. Lans continued to maintain that the standard of care would have been to get cultures during that first week and to continue her antibiotics, but he acknowledged that he could not say whether or not that would have changed her course.

Tommy asked Dr. Lans whether he thought her phlebitis had been managed appropriately. His initial response was that he would have to review her medication and lab tests. When Tommy reminded him that he had testified in his deposition that her phlebitis had been managed appropriately, Dr. Lans, not wanting to get caught in that snare again, quickly retreated and agreed that her phlebitis had, indeed, been managed correctly.

Tommy then submitted to the jury a quotation taken from Artz and Hardy's *Complications in Surgery and Their Management*:

> The location of the ureter makes it liable to injury in almost every pelvic operation, but especially when there is extensive endometriosis or inflammation, when it is displaced by a large uterine or ovarian tumor, or when radical excision of the pelvic organs is performed for cancer. The most common sites of injury are at the pelvic brim and particularly in its lowest four to five centimeters as it turns to enter the bladder and is closely related to the cervix. In spite of the greatest care and knowledge of the anatomic relations, the ureter may be unexpectedly injured. In fact, this may occur more frequently than is usually recognized.

Dr. Lans acknowledged the accuracy of the statement and said he agreed with it.

Tommy made sure the jury was aware of just how much

money Dr. Lans was being paid for his testimony and that he had worked with the Chicago lawyers frequently in the past. His testimony would obviously have been much more believable if he had not been receiving an exorbitant sum of money to give it. I wondered what his opinion would have been about the case if a defense attorney had asked him to review it and testify. I felt certain his testimony would have been markedly different under that circumstance.

When the questioning was finished and Dr. Lans was dismissed, I watched the jurors observing him walk by. I wondered whether they saw him as a truthful physician, courageously standing up for what he thought was just, or as a person motivated by avarice, prostituting his testimony for a fee. I hoped they perceived him to be closer to the latter.

Chapter 20

Wednesday Morning, August 28, 1985

Few were his words, but wonderfully clear.
—Homer

requently, in a medical malpractice trial, expert witnesses who are actively engaged in busy medical practices out of town are asked to testify. It is not possible to predict exactly what day and hour their testimony would naturally occur during the course of the trial, making it difficult for them to arrange their practices unless special consideration is given. For this reason, an agreement is frequently reached between the attorneys involved and the judge, to notify the physician in advance of the time his testimony will be taken and to honor that time even if it means taking the expert out of turn.   Such was the case with our first expert witness, Dr. William Maddox, from Birmingham.   He would be the first witness Wednesday morning, then Hogan would continue his case.

As Dr. Cameron and I walked from the parking lot to the courthouse that morning, we talked about how the case was going.   Dr. Cameron agreed their case was flimsy, at best, but he was worried that the jury might sympathize with Kathy anyway.   I honestly thought we were ahead at that point, even though we had only heard Hogan's side so far, and that we would win if it went to the jury right then. I told Dr. Cameron that I thought Kathy was probably embarrassed now that she had heard what had really happened and was probably sorry she had sued us.   Dr. Cameron chuckled and shook his head, the way he does when he is amused by the naivete of one's thoughts.   He assured me that Kathy was not in the least bit sorry she was dragging us through this ordeal, nor was he as confident as I that we were winning the case.

When we entered the courtroom, we sat down at the table with Tommy and Charlie, watching the jurors' faces as they strolled in.   What I would have given to know just what those fourteen people were thinking!   Had they already decided how they would cast their votes?   Were they like many jurors, making up their minds the first day based on the appearance and mannerisms of the involved parties and the opening statements of the attorneys?

When Dr. Maddox entered the back of the courtroom, Dr. Cameron leaned over and told Tommy that he had made it. Tommy smiled and replied that he and Charlie had been with Dr. Maddox since six o'clock that morning.

Tommy and Charlie were dividing the responsibilities in the case, as is their wont when they work together, so that they can concentrate their energies and therefore be more effective. When Judge Price took his seat, Charlie, who was handling the examination of our expert witnesses, called Dr. Maddox to the witness stand.

Dr. Maddox walked briskly across the room, an air of confidence, yet, at the same time, unassuming humility about him. Tall, handsome, erudite, and articulate, he is the kind of person whose presence commands immediate trust and respect. There was no one in the world whom I would have preferred be there at that time to defend us. I had worked closely with him during my training and had developed the utmost respect for him, both as a person and as a surgeon. I knew the jury would love him.

Charlie, a seasoned veteran in the courtroom, positioned himself between Dr. Maddox and the jury so that Dr. Maddox could comfortably look at the jury when he responded to his questions. I had known of Charlie by reputation for about ten years, and personally for several years; but this was the first time I had seen him in action. He is a large man with slightly rotund features, his blond hair just beginning to thin. He would not be at all out of place cast as a wise and loving father on a television series. Like Tommy, he also is fiercely competitive, abhorring defeat in the courtroom as much as his beloved friend, Bear Bryant, abhorred defeat on the football field.

"Dr. Maddox," he began in a deliberate, low-key manner, carefully enunciating each word, "do you operate on patients with cancer?"

"Yes," replied Dr. Maddox.

"Are you a general surgeon as well?" continued Charlie.

"Yes."

"Give us an idea of how many operations you do or participate in on an annual basis."

"About five hundred," replied Dr. Maddox in a matter of fact manner.

"And how many of those operations are cancer operations?"

"Essentially all."

"So your subspecialty then is cancer surgery?"

"Yes."

"Do you operate on patients who have the same kind of cancer as Ms. Kathy Roberts?"

"Yes."

"Do you teach medical students and residents at the University of Alabama Medical School how to operate on this kind of cancer?"

"Yes."

"Do you manage the postoperative care of cancer patients?"

"Yes."

As Charlie continued his questioning it was apparent that he was thoroughly prepared and knew exactly where he was going. Dr. Maddox was calm and poised as he succinctly answered the questions. He told of his training at Cornell University Medical School, Bellevue Hospital in New York City, and the Memorial Hospital for Cancer and Allied Diseases (now known as the Memorial Sloan-Kettering Cancer Center), one of the leading cancer hospitals in the world. These were impressive credentials for a boy from Abbeville, Alabama.

"While you were at the Sloan-Kettering Memorial Hospital, did you learn about and perform an operation called 'exenteration?'"

"Yes."

"Did the procedure known as pelvic exenteration, which is involved in this case, originate and was it pioneered at Sloan-Kettering Memorial Hospital in New York?"

"Yes, I would say that they did more of it in that period of time, in its early development, than probably any other institution in the world."

"Dr. Maddox, how many surgical cases of pelvic exenteration have you done?"

"It must have been in the hundreds that I've participated in, one way or another."

"Would you give us an estimate of how many?"

"I would say four or five hundred."

In sharp contrast to Dr. Lans, who testified that he had done about fifteen exenterations during his twenty-five year surgical career, Dr. Maddox was truly a leading authority on the procedure. Charlie was methodically pulling some impressive credentials from him. It was apparent to everyone in the room that Dr. Maddox's excellence as a surgeon was exceeded only by his modesty and humility.

"All right, sir," Charlie continued. "Have you done pelvic exenteration for exactly the same type problem that Ms. Kathy Roberts had?"

"Yes."

"Have you written in the medical literature of the world about cancer surgery?"

"I have not been a prolific contributor to the literature," answered Dr. Maddox modestly, "but I have contributed."

"I have counted thirty-six publications," countered Charlie. "Does that sound about right?"

"Yes."

Charlie went on to extract that, in addition to his contributions to textbooks, Dr. Maddox's articles had been published in many of the leading surgical journals. He was also a member of many prestigious organizations, including the Society of Surgical Oncology, one of the top cancer surgery societies in the world.

"Please tell us, Dr. Maddox, what are the problems that the surgeon faces in dealing with a cancer like this, that has perforated through the colon and spilled into the area?"

"Well, colon cancer is common cancer," said Dr. Maddox, obviously relieved that the focus of the discussion had shifted from his credentials to cancer. "Its outlook is based largely on how early it is diagnosed. Obviously, if a cancer of the colon has gone through the wall of the colon, then it's a more advanced cancer. If the cancer perforates and forms an abscess, there is a high chance that cancer cells will be implanted within the wall of the abscess causing the chances of cure by any method to be severely compromised."

Charlie asked Dr. Maddox briefly about Kathy's care up to the time of her second operation, then asked him about problems a surgeon might encounter in the situation that faced us in April.

"In order to encompass the cancer that is left in the pelvis," Dr. Maddox continued, "the surgeon must have a fairly free hand in attempting to remove it. It is a busy place from an anatomical point of view. The genital tract is located there. The urinary tract is located there. The colon is still in place. The tissue in the pelvis is contaminated with cancer cells, so you must plan to take out whatever you have to in order to cure the patient."

"Now would you expect there to be adhesions and scar tissue from the previous infection and surgery?" asked Charlie.

"Yes."

"And what problems, if any, does that present to the surgeon?"

"That means that other organs could be caught down in that abscess. The whole abscess cavity must be considered suspect as far as containing cancer. The scar is formed, which is firm. You could say, 'Well, this is just scar that is healing.' But you have to assume that the scar has cancer cells in it in a situation like this. So, your approach to it is to stay within planes that are outside that tumor and scar."

"Is it a good idea to cut through the cancer or into the cancer?"

"Well, that's tantamount to losing your status for curing the patient."

"Why?" asked Charlie.

"You implant more cells," explained Dr. Maddox. "You have more tissue planes violated, and if tumor cells are spread within the new tissue planes, then you have a bigger problem."

"So if you cut into or through the cancer, you are more apt to spread more cancer. Is that it?"

"Yes," responded Dr. Maddox.

"So how," asked Charlie, "do you avoid cutting into the cancer or through it to keep from spreading cancer?"

"Stay in tissue that is not involved in the scar or the cancer, or in organs that might be in juxtaposition to the scar or cancer," explained Dr. Maddox.

"Do you have to cut through and cut out healthy, normal tissue?" asked Charlie.

"Yes."

"Do you teach that the best way to operate on cancer is to cut healthy and normal tissue that is around the suspected area?"

"You must do it that way," emphasized Dr. Maddox.

"Dr. Maddox, in the process of doing this type of operation, do you cut ureters?"

"Yes, you can cut ureters."

"Do *you* cut ureters?" asked Charlie.

"I've cut them."

"Do you cut them purposely sometimes?"

"Yes."

"Do you cut them sometimes when you don't know that there is a ureter in the scar tissue?"

"Yes."

"And have you done that?"

"Yes."

"Is that necessary for any reason?" asked Charlie.

"Yes. No one cuts a ureter because they want to. It's a simple matter that you have to make commitments at the operating table according to the findings. And unless you make these commitments, then you are not going to cure very much cancer."

"Are you saying that it is necessary to cut ureters sometimes in order to cure cancer?" asked Charlie.

"Yes. The ureter can be involved in the cancer, or in the process of the operation you have to make commitments to make certain cuts with a scissor or a knife, because you are committed to taking the cancer out. If you happen to cut a ureter or something like that, you have to pick up the pieces."

"Do you also have to have a commitment to cut around and out the scar tissue and the mass of adhesions for the same reason that you are taking the cancer out?" asked Charlie.

"Yes."

"And in the process of that, you sometimes cut a ureter?"

"Yes, you do."

Charlie asked Dr. Maddox some questions about the repair of ureters, ascertaining that it is important not to put too many sutures in them, to avoid cutting off the blood supply. Consequently, you expect some leakage of urine between the sutures while they are healing. He asked if Dr. Maddox had an opinion as to whether the ureter had been repaired properly.

"The proof is in the pudding," responded Dr. Maddox. "The ureter worked, so I say it was done properly. They did the little things that are necessary to make it work."

"Dr. Maddox, in your opinion, was it negligence or carelessness or malpractice to cut that ureter under the circumstances they were facing?"

"No."

"Now, Dr. Maddox," Charlie continued, "it's been described in this case that the drainage from Ms. Roberts continued over a period of days and was described as heavy at one time. Is heavy drainage, in a situation like this, a good sign or a bad sign?"

"Well, you would normally expect the drainage to decrease as the postoperative days come along. I think at some day there the drainage was more, and I think everyone's suspicion was that she was leaking some urine. You take cognizance of that, but if things are going well, you do nothing at that point."

"With a patient like this, would you install a Foley catheter after the operation?" asked Charlie.

"Oh, yes."

"Does that have anything to do with whether or not the ureter has been injured or cut?"

"No, that would be done whether the ureter was cut or not."

"You do that on all patients?" asked Charlie.

"All that you do exenterative surgery on."

"Now," Charlie continued, "do urinary tract infections

follow with patients in the hospital who have had catheters in for a period of several days?"

"Most catheters cause some. You have some contamination with catheters in."

"In your opinion, was the urinary tract infection in this patient a serious problem?"

"I don't see anything in the record that says that this patient had a serious urinary tract infection or that she had any invasive infection as a result of the urinary tract."

"In your opinion did the urinary tract infection that she had cause her any serious or permanent problems?" asked Charlie.

"No."

"Did the cut ureter cause her any serious or permanent problems?"

"No."

"Did you notice that she developed a condition called thrombophlebitis?"

"Yes."

"In your opinion, did the cut ureter or the urinary tract infection cause that thrombophlebitis?"

"No."

"What are the usual causes or factors associated with thrombophlebitis?"

"Thrombophlebitis can occur, de novo, in a person who is up walking around — without known cause. This is a little more common in patients who harbor a cancer, but it can occur in other situations. Thrombophlebitis following surgical operations is common — very common."

Dr. Maddox went on to discuss the management of thrombophlebitis and said, in his opinion, it had been managed expertly in Kathy. He thought she lost her leg as a result of the phlebitis and that it could not have been managed any better. In fact, the result would have been the same had she been at University Hospital in Birmingham or at Sloan-Kettering in New York.

"Did you look at the antibiotics that were given to this patient before and after the surgery?" asked Charlie.

"Yes."

"What is your evaluation of the antibiotic therapy in this case?"

"Antibiotics were given preoperatively and, I believe, for two or three days postoperatively. That is a well accepted concept of so-called prophylactic antibiotic use. The longer use of it has some problems at times and is thought not to be necessary."

"Would the fact that the ureter was cut during the surgery change that in any way?"

"No."

"How long do you give antibiotics after surgery like this, even if a ureter is cut?"

"It would vary according to the situation, but in a situation like this, I think that this three days of antibiotics is good."

"Did you notice in the record that Dr. Cameron had originally ordered antibiotics for three days and then after two days Dr. Snider discontinued them?"

" I think that is perfectly within good practice."

"Did the antibiotic program for Ms. Kathy Roberts work satisfactorily for her good?"

"I think so."

"Would there have been any difference in the outcome if she had been put on antibiotics after surgery and kept on antibiotics continually?"

"I don't think so."

"Would she be any better off today, in your opinion?"

"No."

"Would she be any worse off today?"

"She could be, but probably not."

"Did you notice the temperature charts in this case?"

"Yes."

"I will ask you if the temperature, as recorded in those temperature graphs, showed that she ever had any generalized infection, peritonitis, septicemia or anything like that?"

"I couldn't find it in the chart."

"Dr. Maddox, I will ask you if, in your opinion, Dr. Cameron's care of this patient was in all ways within standards of care for surgeons treating patients like this in the United States?"

"Yes."

"Was Dr. Snider's care of this patient within the standards for treating patients like this in the United States?"

"Yes."

"Was Ms. Roberts in the hands of good doctors?"

"Yes."

"What would have happened if she hadn't been in the hands of good doctors?"

"She could very well have lost her life."

Charlie walked quietly to the defendants' table and sat down, allowing the jury a few moments to ponder Dr. Maddox's last words. I could not have been happier with the testimony given.

Chapter 21

Wednesday Morning, August 28, 1985

Cleverness and stupidity are
generally in the same boat
against wisdom.
—J. A. Spender

*A*fter a brief recess, Hogan, who seemed understandably nervous, began his cross examination of Dr. Maddox. His task was to try to discredit a highly credible witness, one who had almost surely engendered the respect of the jury, and the task would not be easy. Again he was functioning without the benefit of a deposition and was going to have to take some shots in the dark, hoping one would hit a weakness. He began by trying to get the jury to believe that Dr. Maddox's motives for being there were either friendship to Dr. Cameron, financial, or blind support for defendants, regardless of the case.   His blind shots were clearly missing their intended mark.

"Are you and Dr. Cameron friends?" asked Hogan.

"We have known one another through our careers. We've had not too much opportunity to be close to one another," responded Dr. Maddox.

"Do you get referral business from him and maybe send referral business down to him?"

Dr. Maddox smiled and said, "Dr. Cameron doesn't have to send very many referrals.   He can take care of the same things I do.   We've talked about problems occasionally — maybe once a year. Not very often."

"Are you going to charge for your time?" asked Hogan.

"I haven't thought about it," responded Dr. Maddox.

"Haven't thought about it?" muttered Hogan, apparently surprised that a witness would give no thought to whether he was to be remunerated for his time.

"Nope," replied Dr. Maddox succinctly, ending that discussion.

"Have you testified in a malpractice case before?" tried Hogan.

"Yes."

"For the defendant?"

"Yes."

"For the plaintiff?"

"Yes."

Had Hogan known the answer to that question he never would have asked it.   He went on to establish that Dr. Maddox had never testified for a plaintiff in Alabama and implied that he would be under extreme pressure if he did so.

He then turned his attention to the case at hand.

"Tell the jury what it means when you say you dissect out the ureters."

"The ureters come from above the pelvis and traverse the pelvis to get to the bladder," explained Dr. Maddox. "If you dissect out the ureter higher up, then you have some idea where it might be going lower down as it gets closer to the bladder and other structures in the pelvis."

"Earlier, when Mr. Stakely was asking you questions, you were talking about adhesions and things like that. Is part of the reason you dissect out the ureter so that you can separate out the ureter from the adhesions and things around it?"

"Yes," answered Dr. Maddox.

"Now," continued Hogan, "you mentioned earlier that you have cut some ureters, and I thought I heard you mention two situations where, number one, the ureters were part of the cancer or were bound up in the cancer. Is that one situation where you cut some ureters?"

"I'm sure I've cut ureters in both situations," said Dr. Maddox.

"Well," said Hogan, "the other situation that I was going to get to was where, I think you said you cut ureters that were bound up in adhesions. Is that the other situation?"

"Yes," replied Dr. Maddox. "It's not that uncommon to have it happen."

"Have you done it?" asked Hogan.

"Yes," replied Dr. Maddox.

"What I want to ask you about, though, is a third situation," said Hogan, confident that he was about to make an important point. "I want to ask you if you've cut a ureter after you have already dissected it out from the adhesions?"

"Yes," replied Dr. Maddox, much to Hogan's dismay.

Hogan was paying a high price for not having deposed Dr. Maddox ahead of time. The questions he was asking would have been good ones for direct examination by *our* attorneys. He would probably never have asked them if he had had any inkling that Dr. Maddox had cut ureters in that situation.

"What if you were to cut the ureter, Dr. Maddox, at a location where you knew where it was and where you had already dissected it out from the surrounding tissues. If you cut the ureter there, is that part of the procedure?"

"It could be part of it," replied Dr. Maddox.

"Okay," said Hogan. "What if it is not associated with any other cancer at that location?" persisted Hogan.

"I think you would have to be there to know the circumstances, and you haven't been there," said Dr. Maddox, as I silently cheered.

"Let's look at the first surgery," he said, referring to the January, 1981, operation. "The cancer that was removed in the first surgery was about six centimeters in size. Is that about right?"

"I don't recall the exact size," said Dr. Maddox.

"Well, assume that it was. Would that be about the size of a tennis ball?" asked Hogan.

"I don't know the dimensions of a tennis ball," said Dr. Maddox.

"About how many inches would six centimeters be?" asked Hogan.

"Two and a half inches."

"Do you recall from the first operation that Kathy was out of the hospital in about a week?" asked Hogan.

"I don't recall that," said Dr. Maddox. "I recall that there were no major complications."

"And the cancer that was removed in April was a little

bit less than three centimeters. Is that right?" asked Hogan.

I could hardly believe what I was hearing. Surely, I thought, Hogan is not going to imply that since the cancer was half as large in April, the operation was half as hard, and she should have been home in half the time.

"I don't recall the exact dimensions," said Dr. Maddox.

"Assume that it was less than three centimeters. And was she in the hospital on this occasion a little over three months?" asked Hogan.

Not only was he making a ridiculous assertion, but he apparently didn't even know she was hospitalized for two months, not three. Kathy had come into the hospital in late April and left in late June, a total of about two months. It seemed to me that Hogan was well on his way to making a fool of himself in front of the jury.

"I thought it was about June that she left," recalled Dr. Maddox.

"It was?" questioned Hogan.

"April, May, June," counted Dr. Maddox. "About two months."

"Maybe that's right," stammered Hogan. "I don't . . . You are right. It was June. Assuming the ——" Hogan stopped in mid-sentence. Apparently he realized how silly his tack was and decided not to pursue that point any further. He changed the subject and began asking about the drainage from the severed ureter.

"Is a quart of urine a day out of what is supposed to be a sewn back ureter — is that *some* urine? Is that what you call *some* urine?" asked Hogan.

"It doesn't take a very big hole to leak out a quart of urine," said Dr. Maddox. "It's a matter of how much is being made by the kidney."

It was an important point that Dr. Maddox was making.

The amount of urine drainage was in large part a function of how much urine her kidneys were putting out which, in turn, was a function of how much she was drinking and how much intravenous fluid she was getting. I was afraid the jury was not following the point, though.

Hogan went on to ask a few questions about infection and thrombophlebitis, not really being able to make any significant points. He then tried to get Dr. Maddox to agree that the ureter was cut at the pelvic brim.

"Iliofemoral thrombophlebitis would be located at around the brim of the pelvis. Is that true, sir?" he asked.

"It might be," answered Dr. Maddox.

"Is that where the ureter was cut in this case?" asked Hogan.

"No," said Dr. Maddox. "I don't think so."

Hogan looked incredulous and began shaking his head as if in disbelief.

"Well, is that —— is your testimony," he asked slowly, emphasizing his words to exaggerate his degree of amazement, "based on an understanding of this record, that the ureter was not cut at the brim of the pelvis?"

"From what I can read and see," said Dr. Maddox calmly, "it was not cut at the brim of the pelvis."

Hogan dropped his legal pad to the table in exasperation, continuing to shake his head in disbelief, hoping, I suppose, that the jury would adopt his attitude.

"That's all I have." he said, as if to communicate to the jury that if Dr. Maddox was going to lie like that, there was no need to waste any more time questioning him.

Charlie quietly arose and walked calmly, deliberately, over to Hogan and handed him a copy of something he was about to introduce into evidence. Turning to Dr. Maddox, he said, "While he is looking at that, were you the first chief of the Department of Surgical Oncology at the University of Alabama?"

"The Section of Oncology within the Division of General Surgery," clarified Dr. Maddox.

"Did you start that?"

"Yes."

"Dr. Maddox, do you expect some elevated temperature following a major operation like this?"

"Yes."

"And did her temperature do about what you would expect it to do following this kind of surgery?"

"Yes."

"Did you notice that when they went back in and operated later that there was no pus in the pelvis?"

"Yes."

"What does that say, if anything about whether or not this lady had an invasive, serious, generalized infection?"

"In my review of the record," said Dr. Maddox, "I never did find a place that I thought the patient had significant bacteremia or septicemia or localized abscess in the pelvis or in the operative area."

"And does the absence of frank pus in the pelvis tend to rule out a generalized serious infection?" asked Charlie.

"You could have it without it," said Dr. Maddox, "but certainly that would be the location that you would expect it to occur and give trouble were it present."

"If there were no pus in the pelvis," asked Charlie, "would that be a reassuring sign?"

"Yes."

"I want to show you what has been marked 'Defendant's Exhibit Two,'" said Charlie, handing Dr. Maddox a copy of the document he had given to Hogan moments before. "It's a radiology report of May 25, 1981, at the time the nephrostogram was done. What is a nephrostogram?"

"A nephrostogram," explained Dr. Maddox, "is putting in dye through a tube that has been placed in the kidney. You place dye in there and let it run down the ureter. They were looking for what we call leakage or extravasation of urine from the site where the ureter had been put together. In other words, they put in a liquid, like water, except it has something in it that will show up on x-ray. That's an easy way to find out where you stand as far as the integrity of the collecting system of the kidney is concerned."

"On May 25, where did the urologist see the dye or the leak coming out of that ureter? What part of the ureter?"

"Fairly low," said Dr. Maddox.

"State whether or not Defendant's Exhibit Two, which was the radiologist's report of the dye test on that ureter, shows where the ureter was cut," said Charlie.

Dr. Maddox picked up the report and read directly from it, "'The contrast media could be seen flowing down the right ureter. There was extravasation' — that means leakage — 'of the contrast media in the area of the surgical clips just above the bladder.'"

"Now," said Charlie, "is 'just above the bladder' the pelvic brim?"

"No," said Dr. Maddox.

"Is it below the pelvic brim?"

"Yes."

"Is that where they were cutting out this mass of adhesions?"

"Yes."

"Thank you," said Charlie, as he turned and took his seat.

Charlie's perfect sense of timing, gained through years of courtroom experience, was showing. He had not introduced the x-ray report during his direct examination of Dr.

Maddox, but had waited until Hogan implied that Dr. Maddox must be lying if he said the chart reflected that the ureter was cut below the pelvic brim. Then he masterfully introduced this document. It had been dictated by a completely unbiased radiologist who was not even peripherally involved in the lawsuit. It had been transcribed during Kathy's hospitalization, long before a suit was filed. There could be no charge that this document was anything other than an accurate, unbiased record of where the leak was in the ureter. It was obvious that the leak was at the point where the ureter had been sewn together and equally obvious that it was sewn together at the point where it had been cut. The report clearly showed that the leak was *"in the area of the surgical clips just above the bladder."*

It seemed to me that Hogan had overlooked that report, or that he was gambling that we had overlooked it when he implied that Dr. Maddox was lying. Hogan should have swallowed it at that point, but instead rose for what turned out to be the *coup de grâce*.

"Is that document that you are looking at an x-ray report?" asked Hogan. "Is that what this is? a nephrostogram?"

"Yes," replied Dr. Maddox.

"And is 'extravasation' a big fancy word that simply means the x-ray technician sees an area of white on what is otherwise a black negative? Is that what that essentially means to a jury, in layman's terms?" asked Hogan.

"Shall I try to explain to the jury what I think it is?" asked Dr. Maddox.

"Sure," said Hogan.

"All right," said Dr. Maddox, "you put the dye in and it leaked out of the ureter at the point where the ureter was put together."

"No," snapped Hogan. "That wasn't my question. I want to know what *extravasation* is."

"Leak," said Dr. Maddox. "I identified that word for them."

"*Extravasation* means leak?" Hogan asked incredulously.

"It's a leak," said Dr. Maddox, "and the dye *extravasates.* It gets out of that viscus into the surrounding tissue."

"But the word *extravasation,* you are saying, means leak?" asked Hogan.

Dr. Maddox looked puzzled, unable to understand what Hogan was driving at.

"That's what I interpreted it as meaning," said Dr. Maddox.

"Well, let's say if we weren't in a lawsuit," persisted Hogan, "what does the word *extravasation* just mean by itself?"

"In surgical jargon," Dr. Maddox said, "it means exactly what it says here. There was leakage of the dye outside of the ureter into the surrounding tissues."

"Well," said Hogan with a cocky air, "let me get the dictionary here."

He walked over to the back table and confidently picked up the dictionary, apparently certain that he was about to discredit this eminent authority. I could not believe that this was happening, but I settled down in my chair and silently chuckled. I knew I was going to enjoy what was coming.

"Do you ever use a medical dictionary, doctor?" asked Hogan, thumbing through the dictionary as he walked back toward Dr. Maddox.

"Frequently," replied Dr. Maddox.

Hogan found the right spot in the dictionary and silently read the definition of *extravasate.* I saw with pleasure the astonishment in his face as he realized that the word was, indeed, defined exactly as Dr. Maddox had said. There he stood in front of the jury with the dictionary, a grenade that had just exploded in his hand. He began to stammer, "All right . . . Okay ——" as he was obviously trying to decide how to get out of this one.

"*Extravasation* means the escape of fluids into the surrounding tissue. That's what it means. Right?" he said, trying to regain his composure.

"I agree with it," said Dr. Maddox.

"Okay," said Hogan, again reading from the fateful x-ray document. "And this says 'the contrast media could be seen flowing down the right ureter'. That's the sentence right above it. Correct?"

"Correct," said Dr. Maddox.

"Then it says, 'there was extravasation of contrast media in the area of the surgical clips just above the bladder,'" floundered Hogan.

"Correct," said Dr. Maddox.

"This sentence follows the other sentence," Hogan stammered.

"Yes." said Dr. Maddox.

"Is that true?" Hogan asked, unable to retreat gracefully from his predicament.

"That's right," said Dr. Maddox.

"That's all I have," said Hogan, blushing as he turned and sat down.

To me, Hogan had looked like a complete buffoon in cross examining Dr. Maddox. I could not help believing that the jury shared that perception. It was becoming increasingly apparent to me that the quality of legal care Kathy was receiving was far inferior to the quality of medical care she had received. Yet, we were the ones who were being charged with negligence. I wasn't sure whether the fault was with Susan

Loggans, Lee DeWald, or Ben Hogan — or perhaps a combination of the three. What seemed apparent was that someone had dropped the ball somewhere along the line. Although I thought her legal case, like her medical case, was nearly hopeless from the start, she at least deserved to have it treated in the best manner possible. It seemed equally apparent that no one would ever be held accountable for those shortcomings, and I resented that. I was being held accountable for an imperfect result. The hospital record had been combed in retrospect looking for possible "errors." If her legal case had been combed from start to finish and the same standards applied, I was confident more "negligence" would have been found in it than in her medical case. But where would one find the lawyer to do the combing and to file the suit?

Chapter 22

> *We judge others according to results;*
> *how else? — not knowing the process*
> *by which results are arrived at.*
> —George Eliot

*H*ogan called Kathy to the witness stand. One of the reasons, I'm sure, that he had taken the case was that he thought she would make a good witness — one who could charm and sway a jury. Perhaps we were about to find out how accurate that assessment had been. To her credit, she did not exaggerate her limp as she walked to the witness stand. I had heard all kinds of stor-

ies of what witnesses have done to gain sympathy from jurors
and was almost expecting her to slip down or lose her leg or
something spectacular like that. Despite the fact that she
had caused me over two years of anguish and countless
sleepless nights, I still could not help feeling sorry for her.
She, too, had been through hell. Thirty years old and strick-
en with cancer, coping with a colostomy and an amputation,
divorced and caring for two small children — how could anyone not feel compassion for her?

Kathy spoke in a soft voice as she answered Hogan's
questions about her education, marriage and career. She
described her graduation from high school, marriage to her
high school sweetheart at age eighteen, and the birth of
her two daughters, aged five and eight. She rambled a little
about the early jobs she had held until Hogan focused her
attention on the Cinderella Cleaning Service she and her
sister had established in April of 1979, a rather industrious
undertaking. They had advertised their new business by
walking around neighborhoods leaving fliers in mailboxes
and doors. Kathy described how she would get down on
her hands and knees and scrub bathrooms, baseboards,
and kitchens — things she would obviously have difficulty
doing now.

In October, 1980, "before the cancer," Kathy went to
work part-time for World Book Encyclopedia, working for
her mother, the district manager. After questioning her
briefly about this employment, Hogan turned his attention to
the operations Dr. Cameron had performed on her. Kathy
explained that the first time she met Dr. Cameron was in
January, 1981, following her first operation. It was then that
he told her she had cancer and that he had performed a colostomy on her. She described what an easy time she had
had after that operation in January and added that she could

live with a colostomy. She described to the jury the ways in which having a colostomy impacts upon everyday activities — bathing, eating, parental responsibilities, etc.

"I have two little girls," she said, "and with little busy people you can't wait — you have to adjust your schedule to theirs."

There was little doubt that Kathy knew the right things to say to the jurors. Surely the parents on the jury could relate to the necessity of adjusting their schedules to those of their children.

Kathy described how Dr. Cameron had seen her in his office following the first operation and had explained the possibility of recurrent cancer and the need for a biopsy. She told the jurors that Dr. Cameron told her the biopsy later showed that she had more cancer and would need another operation. Hogan asked her to relate her recollections of the postoperative period.

"You wake up in intensive care," she said, "and just think, goodness gracious, I do hurt a lot. But that's what there is."

"Do you remember Dr. Snider coming in to see you that first week?" Hogan asked.

"No, but I had a lot of pain medications and things, so if he was there — if the records show he was there, I'm sure he was there."

I wondered if she really didn't remember seeing me that whole week, or was she trying to portray me as being so inattentive that my presence was almost unnoticeable?

After a few more questions, Hogan told her that he wasn't going to ask her much about the hospitalization because they had the records to provide that information. Instead, he began to focus on the personal havoc that ensued in her life after she went home from the hospital. She said that she had lain in bed for two or three weeks before being able to get up. She could not even raise her arm because of the stroke. She had to work with a physical therapist to learn to walk again and with a speech therapist to learn to talk again. She no longer had Cinderella Services. It had to be sold while she was still in the hospital because there was no one to manage it.

"Now, your life has changed in other ways besides your job since this hospitalization. Is that right?" asked Hogan.

Kathy nodded affirmatively and responded, "My life change at home is worse than anything I went through in the hospital." She continued to explain to the jury the frustrating events that were taking place at home following her discharge from the hospital.

"I came from the hospital and David had to start doing everything. He had to earn a living. He was co-manager of a grocery chain here in this city. He emptied my bedpan, washed the girls, fixed dinner, washed the clothes, and washed the dishes. At times he was so exhausted that he would fall asleep on a chair in the den and not hear me ringing the bell when I needed a bedpan.

"So, you know," she said, "there was a lot of frustration that went on in our home, and a lot of tears on both sides were shed."

Ultimately, she explained, her husband left her in August, 1982, fourteen months after her discharge from the hospital. The implication at this point was that there had been a very happy marriage that was destroyed by the handicaps and burdens that she and her family had suffered as a result of her treatment for her cancer.

She continued relating the frustration that she had experienced in learning to cope with using a prosthesis for a leg. She described an experience in a grocery store when her prosthesis slipped off, humiliating her in front of her children and the other shoppers.

"To live with one leg," she added, "when you had won a ribbon for diving one time, to live with one leg when your daughter learns to ride a bicycle ——" Kathy turned toward the jury. "Remember how we all learned? Our mothers or our fathers run ——"

Tommy objected that Kathy was not supposed to be placing herself in the shoes of the jurors, but he was overruled.

"I did not teach my daughter to ride a bike because I couldn't," continued Kathy. "I did not teach her to roller skate because I couldn't — because I can't now. But I could before."

"I guess you don't sleep with your leg, do you?" asked Hogan.

"I asked that question too," responded Kathy. "No, you take it off. If there was an emergency in your house one night, if there was a fire, you could just jump right up out of bed and get your kids. I jump up and put my leg on before I go get mine."

Hogan concluded his examination of Kathy by introducing into evidence and giving to the jury a picture of Kathy with her mother and her two daughters — a picture that showed Kathy standing on one leg without her prosthesis.

Tommy stood and walked to the witness stand, a difficult task before him. The impression that the jurors must have had at this time was that Kathy had had a "marriage made in Heaven" prior to her devastating illness. Nothing could have been further from the truth. Tommy's task was to bring out the truth without seeming unkind to Kathy, who surely had the sympathy of the jury at this point. He began by questioning her in more detail regarding her position at World Book, establishing that, in addition to the receipts she made from her own sales, she also received a commission on the sales of those she supervised.

"So you have been able to do that kind of business for the last several years, have you not?" questioned Tommy.

Again she responded affirmatively.

The questions flowed smoothly and naturally from Tommy as he calmly invaded the delicate sphere relating to the marriage.

"Now, Kathy, your husband's name was David, wasn't it?"

"My ex-husband's name was David, yes."

"And actually, you said that you and he had lived in Demopolis, and Tuscaloosa, and Selma, I think, and Montgomery?"

"Uh huh."

"And y'all had been divorced one time before, hadn't you?" asked Tommy, delicately, his manner and expression almost apologizing for having to ask the question.

"One year after we were married we were divorced for three months and then remarried," said Kathy.

"And you and David had had some problems prior to your having cancer, hadn't you?"

"David and I had had problems no different from any other marriage that has problems from time to time."

Tommy gently proceeded, "One problem was that David's drinking was a problem, wasn't it?"

"David did drink occasionally," Kathy responded.

"And, of course, you are aware that he has given a deposition in this case."

"Uh huh"

"The drinking was more than just drinking occasionally, wasn't it? Wasn't that a problem with you?"

"David could go for long periods of time and not drink," responded Kathy.

"I understand," said Tommy. "But when he did, didn't you and he have some difficulties over his drinking?"

"It was something that I didn't like."

"I understand that you didn't like that. But that caused y'all problems back before you had the cancer, didn't it?"

"He had been drinking before I had cancer."

"Okay. And you had also had a problem where you found out he was seeing another woman, in fact, before you had the cancer."

"Ten years before," Kathy responded.

"And that was in Selma?"

"Right."

"Was that after you had been married, divorced and re-married?"

"Yes."

"Now, Kathy, I'll have to ask you," said Tommy apologetically. "Are you aware that David has said he had trouble after you came home with the fact that, in front of the children, you blamed him for the loss of your leg and for having the stroke?"

"I know David said that."

"Do you deny that you blamed him, or do you think he misunderstood something?"

"There was a big misunderstanding going on at that time."

"But at least you are aware that ——"

"That that went on," agreed Kathy.

"And that David said that is one thing that he couldn't handle — that he felt that you blamed him and told your children that he was to blame?"

"I know he did."

After some questions about Kathy's family history of cancer, Tommy asked her about her experience in the hospital in January.

"I'm sure, Kathy, when you woke up, it was a traumatic thing to know that you had been found to have cancer."

"It was. And then, because our family believes in the Lord so strongly, I was able to handle it. It is something you do think about and make sure you are ready to meet your Saviour."

"You had the colostomy, which is something you certainly didn't expect to have when you went into surgery?" continued Tommy.

"No."

"And Dr. Cameron is the doctor who came in and told you about these things, didn't he?"

"Yes."

"And when he did, you testified in your deposition that he was polite and courteous and responded to your questions, and you liked him, didn't you?"

"Yes, I do. And I still like Dr. Cameron."

"And you knew from that point, as you have said, that you had been found to have a life threatening disease?"

"Yes."

"You did know before the April surgery that Dr. Cameron confirmed that the cancer was still there by doing the biopsy?"

"By doing the biopsy, right."

"Yes, ma'am. Until he confirmed it then, you really didn't know whether you were going to have to have another operation, or what kind of operation, did you?"

"Correct."

"You understood, going in, that it was going to be extensive surgery, didn't you?"

"Yes."

"And, in fact, he even had David come in, and he talked to the two of you and explained that this might interfere with your sex life afterwards?"

"Right."

"So this was understood between you and Dr. Cameron and David, going in, that it was going to be extensive, and these organs would have to be checked, and whatever cancer was there had to be removed?"

"Correct."

"And you certainly understood with this extensive type surgery that death was a certain risk that you faced?"

"I understood it enough to be sure to make peace with my Maker."

And you asked Dr. Cameron to go in and remove all of the cancer, didn't you?"

"To remove the cancer," said Kathy, nodding.

"And that's what you wanted done?"

"Yes."

"And you placed no limits on it?"

"There were no limits."

"Okay. And Kathy, at that time, you knew that this surgery was really your only hope to beat the cancer?"

"Right. I knew when you have cancer you have to have surgery."

"And you acknowledge that Dr. Cameron has removed the cancer?"

"Yes. He has removed the cancer."

"And you acknowledge that he saved your life, do you not?"

"Dr. Cameron has removed the cancer, and Jesus saved my life."

"If Dr. Cameron hadn't removed all of the cancer, do you know whether or not you would be alive today?"

"No, I don't."

"You've talked about your daughters. You have been able to be a mother to them and teach them principles?"

said Tommy, hoping to impress upon the jurors that, despite the tragedies in her life, Kathy was still able to be a mother to her children, a state far preferable to being dead.

Kathy agreed that she had been, in fact, a mother and a father to her children.

Tommy concluded his questioning by establishing the fact that David had visitation rights with the children and made child support payments to Kathy. When the cross examination was completed, Judge Price recessed the proceedings for lunch.

Again, I wondered what was going through the minds of the jurors as I watched them file out of the courtroom. My own thought was that Kathy and Hogan had probably hurt themselves by portraying to the jury a picture of a rosy marriage prior to the April operation, knowing that Tommy knew that not to be the case. Were the jurors thinking, as I, that if she would intentionally mislead them about that point, that she would likely be less than honest about others? I hoped so.

That afternoon Hogan called Kathy's stepfather of seventeen years as his next witness. I couldn't imagine what his testimony would be nor how it would fit into Hogan's overall plan as he answered Hogan's questions about his career. It soon became clear.

"Now the evening after Kathy's second surgery, April 23, were you at the hospital?" asked Hogan.

"Yes."

"Was there an occasion following that surgery when Dr. Cameron came out and explained what had happened in the surgery?"

"Yes, sir."

"Will you just tell the jury what he said that you remember?"

"It appeared that he was very alarmed. He said that he had gotten all the cancer, but 'we made a mistake'. He said 'we made a mistake', and he said this about three times. 'But we've repaired the damage. We cut the ureter.' We didn't know what the ureter was, so he explained to us in language we could understand."

"That's all I have," said Hogan as he turned and walked to his seat.

Tommy rose, walked toward the witness, introduced himself, and proceeded with his cross examination. He established that Dr. Cameron had openly discussed the cut ureter with them, answered all of their questions, and was always courteous and polite throughout the hospitalization.

Hogan called two more witnesses. One had been a friend of Kathy's for fifteen years, and the other had formerly been her minister. Both of them testified that her life had been greatly changed as a result of her cancer and its treatment.

We had no disagreement whatsoever with the contention that Kathy was totally different now than she was in the carefree days of her youth and markedly different than she was before she developed cancer. The issue was whether Dr. Cameron and I had caused this difference through negligence.

Judge Price retired to his chambers to have a discussion with the attorneys. Tommy and Charlie asked for a directed verdict on the grounds that Hogan had presented insufficient evidence to support his claims to even be worthy of the jury's consideration. The motion was denied. After returning to the courtroom, Judge Price informed the jury that the plaintiff had rested its case, and it was now time for the defense to start presenting evidence.

Chapter 23

Wednesday Afternoon, August 28, 1985

> *It is too common for those who have*
> *unjustly suffered pain to inflict it*
> *likewise in their turn with the same*
> *injustice.*
> —Samuel Johnson

When Hogan rested his case, our attorneys faced an important decision. Dr. Cameron and I had already testified by virtue of the fact that we had been called earlier as witnesses. However, Tommy had not had an opportunity to question Dr. Cameron on the witness stand. Dr. Morrow had arrived at the courthouse, interrupting Dr. Cameron's testimony before

Tommy had examined Dr. Cameron. If our own attorneys did not call Dr. Cameron back to the witness stand, Hogan could not get another shot at him. Hogan had been at a little of a disadvantage in questioning him the first time. He had not been present for Dr. Cameron's deposition and, consequently, did not know how he would react to questioning. Hogan had been unable to rattle him or destroy his credibility earlier in the week. Presumably, Hogan had learned a little the first time around and might be more effective if given another opportunity. The idea of not giving Hogan another chance was certainly appealing, but not appealing enough to deny the jury the opportunity to hear Dr. Cameron's side of the story again. Tommy and Charlie thought it was important to let the jury get to know, as much as possible, the type of person Dr. Cameron is. He was, therefore, called back to the witness stand.

Tommy asked Dr. Cameron to tell the jury about his background, beginning with his home town of Faunsdale, Alabama, a town so small it did not even have a high school. He told how he did his training at the Mayo Clinic and served in the United States Army before coming to Montgomery to practice in August, 1949. Tommy made it a point to get Dr. Cameron to tell how he and Dr. Till had begun doing pelvic exenterations shortly thereafter on patients who were referred to the State Tumor Clinic. The patients had no financial resources, so Dr. Cameron and Dr. Till operated on them without charging anything.

After a few more background questions, Tommy gave Dr. Cameron a copy of Defendants' Exhibit Two, the x-ray report of the nephrostogram, and had Dr. Cameron read it again to the jury.

"The contrast media could be seen flowing down the right ureter. There was extravasation of the contrast media in the area of the surgical clips just above the bladder."

"Did you use surgical clips in your posterior pelvic exenteration?" asked Tommy.

"Yes, sir."

"And what do you use those for?"

"Primarily to control bleeding," said Dr. Cameron.

"All right, would these surgical clips, that are being described in this report, have been in the area where the adhesions and cancer was being removed?" asked Tommy.

"Yes, sir."

"All right, sir, and he describes these 'down in the area of the bladder'. Is that right?"

"Just above the bladder," agreed Dr. Cameron.

"And were the cancer and the adhesions in that area just above the bladder?" asked Tommy.

"Yes, sir."

"All right, sir. And why would there have been extravasation of the contrast material in that area?" asked Tommy.

"This is where we sewed our cut ends of the ureter together," explained Dr. Cameron. "They had not quite healed, and they were leaking out through the anastomosis."

"All right, would that indicate to you the location of the cut?"

"Yes, sir."

I hoped the jury was following this rebuttal of Hogan's contention that the ureter had been cut way up at the pelvic brim, and that they understood that this had been written by unbiased people over four years earlier. I also hoped that they were recalling that Dr. Lans had said in his deposition that the ureter had been cut in its lower third (which is the part just above the bladder). Only after Hogan was on the case did Dr. Lans decide the ureter was cut at the pelvic brim.

"Now, referring to your operative note of April 23, 1981,"
Tommy continued, "are those clips that are referred to on
that x-ray in the area where you reported in this note that
'everything in the pelvis was pretty well tightly bound
down?'"

"Well, they are in one of those areas. The whole pelvis was
pretty well fixed and so forth."

"Now do you also, after you remove the adhesions and
cancer, submit what you remove for examination?"

"Yes, sir."

"Who do you submit that to?"

"That goes to the pathologist."

"The pathologist," repeated Tommy. "I'll show you what
is already in the record in evidence — the laboratory report
of surgical pathology. Is a pathologist still another kind of
doctor?"

"That's right."

"All right. In this report it states, 'This entire area, however, is a mass of adhesions and hemorrhage, and a discrete
mass lesion is not identifiable'. Is that consistent with the
material you gave the pathologist?" asked Tommy.

"It certainly is," said Dr. Cameron.

"And what does that mean, please sir?"

"It means he is having a hard time knowing what it is, even
looking at it and dissecting it out himself."

"This is, of course, after it's already out of the body?"

"After it's already out of the body," confirmed Dr. Cameron.

"Dr. Cameron, there has been reference to your having
gone to Europe after the surgery. Could you tell us the purpose of that trip?"

"Well, at the time that all this was going on, my wife also
had terminal cancer of the colon. One of her last requests

was that she would like to make a trip to Europe. She seemed to be strong enough at the time so we went for a week and, fortunately, made it back."

"Did she die sometime after you made it back?"

"She died May 24th."

"Now, during that time you had how many partners?"

"I had four partners at that time."

"All right, sir, and Dr. Snider was one of your partners who assisted you in this surgery?"

"That's true."

"And did he follow Kathy postoperatively?"

"Yes, he did."

"And did you have any hesitancy to allow him to follow Kathy postoperatively?"

"Oh, not at all."

"Based on what all you have seen of the records, and you have heard his testimony as to the way he handled her, do you have any disagreement or criticism of the way he followed Kathy and handled her?"

"No, sir."

"All right, now, Dr. Cameron, we have heard about thrombophlebitis occurring in this case. Does the fact that thrombophlebitis follows an operation necessarily mean that there has been infection after the operation?"

"No, sir."

"Are you saying that an operation leads to it even when a patient has no postoperative infection?"

"It certainly can."

"All right, now, does infection always cause thrombophlebitis?"

"No, sir. As a matter of fact, we have a good example right here."

"What is that?"

"Well, in January when I operated on Kathy, she had a great big old pelvic abscess, obvious infection, and yet she didn't get thrombophlebitis."

"Now on the 8th when you detected the first clinical signs, leg swelling, what did you do to check further about thrombophlebitis?"

"Well, I got a venogram and this showed an obstruction in the iliofemoral system."

"Did you treat the thrombophlebitis?"

"Yes, sir."

"What did you treat it with?"

"We used *Heparin*."

"All right, sir, is that the standard, recognized treatment for thrombophlebitis?"

"Yes, sir."

"Now, how did Kathy do after the 8th, after that treatment was started?"

"Well, for a few days she did very well. The leg became smaller. She had had a little temperature, the 7th and 8th, I think, when this thing was going on. We put her on *Heparin*, and her temperature came down. She felt better. It looked like her leg was smaller and softer — less painful. It looked like things were going along very very well."

"All right. Did things change for the worse at some point?"

"Oh, very definitely."

"And when was that?"

"On the 15th of May."

"I noted in here on the progress notes you wrote on May 15th, you wrote a question about *Heparin*. Do you recall that?"

"Yes, sir."

"What did you mean by 'reaction to *Heparin*?'"

"There are certain reactions to *Heparin* in which you get a sort of an adverse reaction. Instead of being a beautiful anticoagulant like it's supposed to be, it might even lead to thromboses."

"So when you are treating with *Heparin,* are you saying that in some people it may do the reverse of what it's supposed to do?"

"Sometimes."

"Is that frequent or infrequent?"

"That is quite rare."

"All right, on the 15th, did you call in any additional doctors?"

"Yes, sir, I did."

"What specialties did those doctors have?"

"Well, I called in a pulmonary doctor, and I called in Dr. Ed Givhan."

"What is his specialty?"

"He is a hematologist."

"What does that deal with?"

"He deals with the blood. The reason, primarily, for calling Dr. Givhan in was the fact that this patient had turned up that day, when we got our lab reports back, with a very low platelet count of eighteen thousand."

"And a pulmonary man — what's his specialty?"

"The lungs."

"Now, was it suspected that she was having clots to her lungs?"

"That was my first impression at that time."

"Dr. Cameron, did any of the consultants you called in say that they thought that her problems at that time, on the 15th, were related to the cut ureter?"

"No, sir."

"And was sepsis considered as a possibility as well at that time?"

"It sure was."

"All right, sir. And did you actually investigate that as a possibility?"

"We certainly did."

"Tell us how you went about investigating the question of whether there was an infection causing her problem."

"While Kathy was in bed in the intensive care unit, I took a glove and broke through my sutures in the vagina, so I could get my finger into the pelvis. I wanted to know whether she had any frank pus in there like she had the first time back in January. I didn't get any."

"All right, sir. Did you stop at that, or did you investigate further?"

"Well, Kathy continued to be ill. There still was this awful possibility of pulmonary emboli and the *Heparin* not working right and having more pulmonary emboli, so, on the 17th, sick as she was, we took her up to surgery."

Dr. Cameron described how he and Dr. Ingalls had looked throughout her abdomen, particularly in the area of the pelvis, for any pus when they tied off her vena cava. Finding no pus inside her abdomen, Dr. Cameron went below and opened up the vagina to be certain there was no pus there either, and there was none.

"Now," Tommy continued, "based on that examination on May 16th and the operation where you looked into the pelvis, can you tell us today whether Kathy Roberts had any infection at all in the pelvic area?"

"I couldn't find any, and I tried hard."

"Did you observe any, Dr. Cameron?"

"No, sir."

"And if she had had an infection from the cut ureter, would it have been observed or observable in the pelvis?"

"I think it certainly would have."

"Dr. Cameron, in your opinion, did the thrombophlebitis Kathy developed relate in any way to the cut ureter?"

"No, sir."

"Did her stroke relate in any way to the cut ureter?"

"No, sir."

"Could it, anatomically or medically, based on what you found in this case?"

"No, sir."

"Dr. Cameron, in all aspects of your treatment — January, April, follow-up care after April — of Kathy Roberts, did you use your best medical care, skill and judgment in every decision you made and every operation you undertook and everything you did?"

"I tried to."

"Did you?"

"Yes, sir."

"Dr. Cameron, when you described how you cut out the cancer and adhesions and scar tissue to this jury, and here today, can you tell us whether you could have prevented cutting the ureter on April 23, 1981?"

"No, sir."

"And in your way of using the English language, did you try to report accurately in that operative note how everything happened that day?"

"Yes, sir."

"You used the word *unfortunately* in that operative note. Why did you use that word?"

"Well, you don't like to do things like cutting a ureter. That *is* unfortunate."

"And did you put that right in the operative note?"

"Yes, sir."

"Well, by using that, did you mean you could have prevented it before you cut it?"

"No, sir."

"Did you intend to convey that to Mr. Hogan or anybody else?"

"No."

"Did you tell the family of Kathy Roberts that you made a mistake, or did you tell them what you put in the operative note?"

"I don't remember. That's been a long time ago. I certainly know I went out and talked to the family. There is a surgical lounge outside surgery at the Baptist Hospital. I remember going out there and talking to a large number of people and telling them, basically, what we did in the surgery. I'm not sure if I said 'mistake.' It doesn't sound like me, really. 'Unfortunately' sounds a little bit more like what I think I might say, but it's hard to be sure now."

"Dr. Cameron, do you know of anything you could have done differently to have prevented Kathy's developing thrombophlebitis and having her leg amputated, or to have prevented her from having that stroke?"

"No, sir."

As Tommy was sitting down and Hogan was getting up to cross examine Dr. Cameron, I glanced at the jurors, hoping to glean something of their reaction toward Dr. Cameron. There was nothing there, or at least I could not perceive any clues in their faces. It was hard for me to imagine anyone not liking him, or not being impressed with his homespun manner of speaking. I wished that I could be more like him on the witness stand. I wondered if I came across to them as arrogant or aloof. I again resented having to wonder what people were thinking of me. The issue in question was not, or at least should not have been, personalities, but whether or not we had been negligent.

"If I understand — well, maybe I don't," began Hogan.

"Let's just make sure, doctor. Are you now trying to tell the jury that the place that you cut the ureter was not, as Dr. Morrow testified, at the pelvic brim?"

"It was not cut at the pelvic brim," responded Dr. Cameron.

"If it had been cut at the pelvic brim in this operation, would you agree that that would have been unnecessary?" asked Hogan.

"I think it might depend a little bit on what the situation was at the pelvic brim," said Dr. Cameron.

"I am talking about this operation, after you had dissected out the ureters, separated them out, if you had then cut the ureter at the pelvic brim, would you agree that that would have been unnecessary in order to remove the cancer?"

"Are you asking if I had dissected the ureter out so I could see it above and below, and then picked it up and cut it, would that have been unnecessary? Is that basically what you are saying?"

"Yes."

"It would have been unnecessary," agreed Dr. Cameron.

"Thank you," said Hogan. "Now, in the record, the jury, when they consider this case will see a word called 'sepsis' or they will see 'septic embolism' or they will see 'CVA, septic in origin'. What does *sepsis* mean?"

"It's a form of infection."

"And is it your position in this case that Kathy did not have sepsis?"

"You know, I can't absolutely say that. We looked for it, but we did more than look for it. We treated it. We treated it with numerous antibiotics. I really can't say that she had no sepsis," responded Dr. Cameron, remembering Tommy's admonition not to fight the sepsis theory too hard. "I can state that the areas we checked did not show evidence of sepsis."

"I guess that last month before your second wife died must have been a trying time for you."

"Yes, sir."

"Doctor, when you are in a situation like that where you have something like that and a physician has that kind of a problem on the home front, I suppose that it can affect the attention that you give to patients that are depending on you. Is that something that you do recognize from time to time?"

"Are you asking if I think it affected my care of Kathy?"

"Let's just use the hypothetical for the moment without getting into your situation. When a physician has a problem like was going on in your home, do physicians recognize that that can affect the quality of care, at least for a brief time, that they are giving their patients?"

"Well, you know, it's pretty hard to answer in a total negative, isn't it, really? I had the advantage of having four partners at the time, and we had talked about this very same problem that you're bringing up. If there had been any problem, they were supposed to look and see and help out and take care. I really think, in our circumstances, we were pretty well covered as far as this sort of business was concerned."

"I understand," said Hogan. "I have nothing further."

Tommy stood up and walked back toward the witness stand.

"Dr. Cameron," he said, "I have one question. How long have you been doing surgery down in the pelvis?"

"Let's see — thirty-six years."

"Thirty-six years. And do you know what a ureter looks like?"

"I sure do."

"Is this the first one that you had ever seen?"

"No, sir."

"In that surgery, did you dissect out and look at it and cut it?"

"No, sir."

"Did you see it before you cut it?"

"Well, we saw the upper part of it where we had dissected it out."

"And is that what you reported you dissected out, in your operative note?"

"Yes."

"Did you see it at the point where you cut it?"

"No, sir."

"Why not?"

"Well, it was bound up in a lot of this old stuff we have been talking about. We were trying to get back to the wall of the pelvis to get all this tissue out that might have contained cancer, and it was sticking against the wall of the pelvis. The deeper you get, the harder it is to see down there. We didn't see it. It's kind of like Dr. Maddox said this morning. Somewhere along the line you have to make up your mind as to whether you are going to divide this or not. And sometimes you have to. We did. And, unfortunately, it was the ureter."

Tommy sat down and up came Hogan for a final round of questions.

"Is Dr. Morrow's specialty the part of the human body that includes the ureter?" asked Hogan.

"Dr. Morrow is a urologist, and he certainly works on the ureter. Yes, sir."

"Would Dr. Morrow be at least as qualified as you in recognizing what part of the ureter had been cut when he looked at it?"

"No, sir."

"He wouldn't be as qualified as you?"

"Dr. Morrow, as I remember his testimony yesterday, was in an operation and he was fifteen minutes before he got in our operating room. By that time, we had gone past the site of injury and had begun to dissect out the lower part. So, by the time Dr. Morrow came, we had two ends of the ureter. The whole area was surrounded by lap packs and we had the ureter out and were getting ready to repair it. Dr. Morrow said it was cut at the pelvic brim. I heard him. But there was no way, really, for him to tell at that time where the pelvic brim was."

"I have nothing further, Judge," said Hogan as he sat down.

Judge Price turned to Tommy and asked who the next witness would be. It was only mid-afternoon, but we had not anticipated calling another witness that day.

"Our next witness is Dr. Orr from Birmingham," said Tommy, "and he will be here the first thing in the morning. We thought that their evidence would go through today."

Judge Price looked displeased.

"That's what we were told," added Charlie.

"We were told it would take the rest of the day, and we have him coming to start at nine o'clock," said Tommy.

Judge Price sat for a moment pondering, as if he were considering forcing us to omit Dr. Orr's testimony and go on to the closing arguments.

"Judge, we just got up to bat," pleaded Tommy.

"All right," said Judge Price. "In the morning both sides have all their witnesses standing right outside of the door."

"Yes, sir," said Tommy.

"We will," agreed Hogan.

Both of them knew full well that they didn't have any witnesses other than Dr. Orr to line up at the door.

I was relieved to be ending the day early. The trial had been going on for three days and I was mentally and physically exhausted. I never realized before that I could get so fatigued by sitting all day. I could not begin to fathom how anyone could endure a trial that lasted for weeks or months.

Tense and fractious, I arrived home that night wanting only to be left alone. I didn't even feel like talking to Pam, but somehow managed to start a fight with her — one of the few we have had before or since. It was as though all of the frustration, the resentment, the anger that had been building since the lawsuit was filed had finally exceeded the critical mass. I exploded. Torrents of hostility spewed forth, directed toward the one who deserved them the least. I yelled at Pam as I have never yelled at anyone before. She stood there for a moment quivering, her eyes reflecting the terror of one who encounters a savage beast, then quickly escaped the room in tears.

My God in Heaven! What is this trial doing to me? I thought. *Will it totally destroy me before it is over?*

I desperately needed to reestablish harmony with Pam, who had been supporting me day and night. The outburst had been so alien to anything we had known before, we would both need to analyze it, discuss it, and understand it before we could lay it to rest. No simple apology would suffice. Yet, I also had a strong, but conflicting desire to just escape from the agony of it all — to sleep, and let nature knit my "raveled sleeve of care." The pull of these opposing needs stretched me even thinner, almost to the point of snapping. Exhausted, I fell into bed. It was only seven o'clock but, without eating supper, I cried myself to sleep.

Chapter 24

Thursday Morning, August 29, 1985

> *Not only is there an art in knowing*
> *a thing, but also a certain art in*
> *teaching it.*
> —Cicero

 hursday morning found me depleted of almost all of my reserves. Fortunately, Pam understood the unprecedented outburst the night before had been caused by the extreme stress that I was under, and she was gracious in her forgiveness. However, a fitful night of sleep had left me as exhausted as I had been the night before. Had the morning not held the prospect of a favorable witness, I am not certain I could have made it out of bed.

Dr. James Orr was an outstanding young academic surgeon from the University of Alabama School of Medicine in Birmingham. He was outraged that charges of negligence had been filed against us when, in his review of the chart, the care seemed excellent in a very complex case. Though he knew neither Dr. Cameron nor me, he devoted a considerable amount of his time to the laborious process of going through the details of the medical record in order to prepare himself to be an excellent witness. His keen mind enabled him to find points in the chart that strongly supported our position — points that even we had missed.

During Charlie's examination I was impressed as I heard Dr. Orr's credentials for the first time. He had attended undergraduate school and medical school at the University of Virginia, receiving honors at each, and was named outstanding teaching resident during his training in Obstetrics and Gynecology at the University of Alabama. Although that training alone had enabled him to become board certified as a gynecologic surgeon, he had completed an additional two year fellowship in female cancer surgery before joining the faculty in Birmingham. A prolific writer, he had already published fifty papers in the medical literature in the last five or six years, four of them on the subject of pelvic exenteration. He had also written a chapter in a textbook on pelvic exenteration and had ten to twelve additional articles which had been accepted for publication over the next couple of years. He was truly an authority on pelvic cancer and its surgical treatment.

Dr. Orr, an instinctive educator, had brought several large drawings done by the Medical Illustrations Department at the University of Alabama to aid in his description of what had transpired in Kathy Roberts' case. He used the drawings to illustrate to the jury normal pelvic anatomy, the relationship of the ureters to other pelvic structures, and the tissues removed during pelvic exenteration.

Dr. Orr confirmed the previous testimony concerning the need for extensive, radical surgery, and estimated the mortality rate from the operation to be 15-20 percent at many institutions. He also concurred that the likelihood of long term survival in a case like this was only 10-15 percent. Charlie had Dr. Orr explain to the jury the location of the original cancer in relationship to the pelvic organs, and established that the January operation would have, of necessity, left scar tissue at, above, and below the pelvic brim. Dr. Orr explained that it would by no means be careless or negligent to cut a ureter under the circumstances of this case. He explained the principles involved in accurately repairing a ureter, adding that a necessary part of the repair included leaving a temporary drain in place. He then discussed the results of some research he had done on patients who had had pelvic exenteration, noting that the drainage averages about fifteen ounces a day and normally increases over the first five or six days.

"We have seen women who haven't had an injury, who haven't had an infection, who haven't had problems, drain as much as seven times that much fluid. So, instead of fifteen ounces, we are talking about ninety-five or a hundred ounces a day," said Dr. Orr.

I hoped the jurors remembered that Hogan and Dr. Lans had said the increasing drainage over the first few days was a sign of infection — an assertion completely devoid of any basis in fact. Dr. Orr had researched that drainage in detail and found that it was *normal* for it to increase during the first week. In fact, some women with no infection or injured ureter had far more drainage than Kathy.

"Why do they drain all that?" asked Charlie.

"This raw area," explained Dr. Orr, "this area that's been denuded from the surgical procedure in an attempt to remove the cancer, is exactly that. It's all raw. It takes time to heal, and it oozes fluid continuously."

"You expect it to?"

"Yes, sir."

"So you expect a lot of drainage in the first week?"

"I do."

"Did you study the medical reports on Ms. Roberts in connection with her drainage through her Jackson-Pratt?"

"I did. Yes, sir."

"And was her drainage more than you would expect, less than you expect, or what you would expect?"

"I would say that the amount of drainage after that type of surgical procedure could be interpreted as normal in many circumstances. We have had women who have put out two and three times that much fluid without anything else occurring, and then recover after the operative procedure."

"Do you culture the drainage from the Jackson-Pratt?" continued Charlie.

"No, sir. I do not," said Dr. Orr.

"Why not?"

"Both at our institution and from surgical departments at Pittsburgh, we have looked at the results of cultures on the Jackson-Pratt drainage. The information from Pittsburgh was just recently reported. Twenty percent or more of the cultures are going to be positive regardless of what's happening inside the abdomen, and there is no relationship between what we grow, if we grow anything, and what happens to the patient in the long run."

"Dr. Orr, in your opinion, was the handling of the Jackson-Pratt and the drainage by Dr. Cameron and Dr. Snider and these other doctors appropriate and good?"

"Yes, sir."

"What is a Foley catheter and why do you use it?"

"A Foley catheter is a catheter that drains the bladder. After pelvic exenteration the bladder doesn't work well because the nerves to the bladder are all coming through these tissues and they have been cut in order to get clearance around the cancer. A Foley catheter is there to make sure that the bladder drains."

"Did Ms. Roberts need a Foley catheter?"

"I think after this operation women need a Foley catheter."

"Now do you see some urinary tract infection with patients who have been on a Foley catheter for a number of days?"

"Once a woman has the Foley catheter in place for three, four, five days, there is almost always colonization, that is, there are bacteria there. I think an important thing about this situation is colonization does not equal infection. Almost all women who have a Foley catheter for any extended amount of time have some chronic bacteria in that bladder."

"Do you have patients with a urinary tract infection from a Foley catheter?"

"I do have patients that have urinary tract infections, but the majority of those patients have colonization. One gets into some problem when we go to treat that area. These bacteria follow their ability to try to survive and develop ways to become resistant to antibiotics. If one gives an antibiotic, the bacteria can become resistant and then make it even more difficult to treat a recurring problem."

"Was the bacteria in Ms. Roberts' urinary tract system correctly and appropriately managed and treated by these Montgomery doctors?"

"I think so. Yes, sir."

"Now, Dr. Orr, in your opinion, did the cut ureter cause in any way the thrombophlebitis she got later?"

"No, sir."

"Did it cause the stroke she had later?"

"No, sir."

"Did the bacteria in the urinary tract from the Foley catheter cause the thrombophlebitis or the stroke?"

"No, sir."

"What, in your opinion, was the cause of the stroke?"

"I believe that the stroke, or vascular accident, that occurred was probably related to a reaction to the medication that was being given. *Heparin* has to be given because if the blood clots break off and go to the lungs, that's a potentially fatal situation. In addition to blood thinning, the use of this drug may have an effect on the blood platelets. I believe that the vascular accident was probably related to what we call *Heparin* induced thrombocytopenia, or *Heparin* induced low platelet counts."

"She had to have the *Heparin*?"

"She did."

"Was it the fault of Dr. Cameron or these doctors that she reacted to the *Heparin* that she had to have?"

"No, sir. It wasn't."

"In your opinion, did Dr. Cameron and Dr. Snider exercise good care with this patient in all respects?"

"Yes."

"In your opinion, was her life saved because of their skill and good work?"

"Yes, sir."

Charlie walked over to where Dr. Cameron and I were sitting, leaned over and asked if we knew of anything else that should be asked. We did not, so he turned the witness over to Hogan for cross examination.

Hogan introduced himself to Dr. Orr and began his questioning.

"Are you being compensated for your time here at court this morning?"

"I would suspect that I will be reimbursed for my time," replied Dr. Orr.

"Have you thought about how much you might charge for that?"

"I have not thought about it nor discussed it."

"It was not something that entered into your thought as part of your coming down here and testifying, was it?" asked Hogan.

"I'm a physician and an educator," replied Dr. Orr, obviously annoyed at the implication that money might be a factor in his testimony. "No, sir. It wasn't."

I hoped that the jury had noticed the sharp contrast in this testimony and that of Dr. Lans. Dr. Lans knew exactly how much he charged for court appearances, depositions, etc. His fee was of vital importance to him. Dr. Orr would have been there testifying in exactly the same manner even if he were not going to be paid a penny.

"Now one of the things that you talked about," Hogan continued, "is this procedure called the posterior pelvic exenteration. We talked about 'in many institutions'. What is the death rate from operations there where you are?"

"Nine point nine percent," responded Dr. Orr succinctly.

It was an important point, and I was glad Hogan had asked it. Even at the University of Alabama, the Mecca, where probably more pelvic exenterations are done than anywhere in the world, the chance that a woman would die just from the magnitude of the operation itself was one in ten. Surely the jury was beginning to be impressed with the formidable task that had faced us.

In his next series of questions, Hogan attempted to establish that the cancer that was removed in April was, in fact,
present at the January operation. Of course, the cancer almost surely was present at least in a microscopic stage at
that time. However, none of the witnesses — not Dr. Lans, or
even Dr. Williams from Sarasota — had implied in any way
that more could have been done during the January operation. It seemed to me that Hogan, by innuendo, was attempting to plant that seed of doubt in the minds of the
jurors, and there was nothing to keep him from doing just
that.

Hogan established with Dr. Orr that iliofemoral thrombophlebitis could extend in the vein near the pelvic brim.
This fact is true in any case of iliofemoral thrombophlebitis
and is completely unrelated to the fact that the ureter crosses
that location. Yet Hogan was trying to get the jury to believe that the ureter was cut at the pelvic brim and the
thrombophlebitis was located there; therefore, the two were
causally related.

I sat there and pondered how unfair it was to be asking a
group of people to decide the veracity of this assertion when
they do not have the knowledge or educational background to
do so. I felt that there must be a better way — a way that
would minimize the chance of misleading someone rather
than inviting it. Perhaps, I thought, some type of erudite
panel should decide these issues rather than juries. That type
of system would almost surely be more predictable and
equitable than a jury system, and it would certainly insure
more expeditious and reasonable judgments for plaintiffs,
with more money ending up in their hands and less in the
hands of attorneys. My mind wandered a bit as I contemplated how such a system would work. The members of
this panel would not sit passively in a box, unable to ask

questions if they were not following what was being said, but would be active inquisitors, seeking the truth. Obviously, the panel could not be composed of medical personnel alone, but at least one unbiased medical person, expert in the field in question, would seem essential. I envisioned adding a professor of chemistry, or biology, or physics, depending upon the charges, and probably an impartial representative of the legal profession.

I caught myself day dreaming, and my mind returned to the courtroom. I realized that Hogan was getting better as the week wore on.

"Was it necessary, Dr. Orr," he asked, "in order to remove the cancer in the second surgery, to cut the ureter at the pelvic brim?"

Hogan was using a clever ploy by asking two questions in one, hoping to lull the witness into implicitly agreeing with his premise. He, no doubt, wanted Dr. Orr to focus on whether it was necessary to cut the ureter and not realize that he was tacitly agreeing that the ureter was cut at the pelvic brim.

"In a hypothetical case," responded Dr. Orr, "It's often necessary to cut a ureter at, above, or below the pelvic brim. In this case the tissues were so obliterated that those areas made it very difficult to dissect around the ureter."

"Well, I am still not clear. In this case, of course, you weren't there. Dr. Cameron was there. You are here to help him. In your judgment, was it necessary in order to remove the cancer, to cut the ureter at the pelvic brim?"

"In the situation that's described in the operative note, I can see that ureter being cut easily. As you said, I wasn't there and have to reconstruct the situation. It may have been necessary."

"Do you understand that the pelvic brim was where it

was cut? Is that your understanding of it?"

"I understand that from the operative note it appears that the ureter was cut around the pelvic brim. I also understand that the leaks that were described later, that is, on the x-rays, seemed to be somewhat lower than the pelvic brim. It was just above the bladder, or just around surgical clips that Dr. Cameron clearly describes using for adhesions. So I believe it was from the pelvic brim down and not above the pelvic brim."

"In fact, wasn't this ureter cut, Dr. Orr, as Dr. Cameron was dividing the peritoneum along the pelvic brim?"

"That would be a place where the injury could occur."

"But wasn't that exactly what the operative note said?"

"May I see the operative note?" asked Dr. Orr.

"Sure," said Hogan, handing him a copy.

Dr. Orr studied the note a moment than replied, "The operative note does describe 'along the brim of the pelvis.'"

"I want to go on to something else," said Hogan. "Have you ever heard of a book called *Complications in Surgery and Their Management* by Hardy?"

"I have seen the book."

"How have you seen it used?" asked Hogan.

"Particularly in relationship to a section on fluids and fluid replacement in women who have had major surgery."

"Well, have you relied upon this book?" asked Hogan.

"No, sir, other than that previously noted use for fluid therapy after surgery."

"Well, do you consider the book since you have relied on at least part of it, an authoritative and accepted medical book?"

This was a key question for Hogan. In order to introduce the book as evidence and quote from it, he had to get Dr. Orr to agree that it was authoritative. And he did.

"I would have to say that it's authoritative in that Dr. Hardy has his name on it," replied Dr. Orr, much to Hogan's pleasure.

Hogan smiled as he turned to Judge Price and said, "We offer this book."

"I want to ask you some questions here," said Hogan. "Chapter One deals with infection and fever in the surgical patient. Would you agree with this statement? 'A culture with greater than one hundred thousand bacteria per milliliter of urine requires treatment.'"

"No, sir," said Dr. Orr. "In a situation ——"

"You answered my question," interrupted Hogan. He was clearly more effective now than earlier in the week when he allowed witnesses to ramble.

As Hogan continued, Dr. Orr disagreed with every question he read, and he did so honestly. The points were all controversial and many authors, equally as authoritative as Dr. Hardy, shared Dr. Orr's philosophy. However, it was an effective maneuver by Hogan to put him in the uncomfortable position of disagreeing with every point read from a book that Dr. Orr, moments earlier, had called authoritative.

When Hogan finished his cross examination, Charlie walked to the witness stand for a brief redirect examination.

"Dr. Orr, just a couple of things. Let me ask you about a statement out of this book you said you didn't agree with. 'The culture with greater than a hundred thousand bacteria per milliliter of urine requires treatment.' Why don't you agree with that?"

"We know that five percent of women who walk around will have that many organisms in their urine. There is no evidence that treatment or lack of treatment changes anything. If one uses an antibiotic, one has to be very careful. I think in this particular instance we see that antibiotics were used at one time with an organism that was sensitive. The Enterobacter was sensitive to a drug called *Geocillin.* Weeks later, the same Enterobacter was resistant to that drug."

"Is that bad?"

"That's bad. That creates organisms that are super organisms. It gives us an inability to treat those patients if they get infected with those kinds of organisms."

"And is that why you don't want to give antibiotics unnecessarily?"

"That's correct."

"And is that the current thinking in 1985 on antibiotic therapy?"

"Yes, sir."

"Do you recommend preoperative antibiotics for a short time?"

"I use preoperative antibiotics for a short time."

"And is that what they did here?"

"Yes, they did."

"Now, after surgery, how long would you have kept this patient on antibiotics before you discontinued it?"

"I would have probably only used three doses of antibiotics. In the past, when we started using these antibiotics, we started out using them for a week or ten days, and then people started looking at it and saying, 'Gosh! That's giving these women a lot of risk!' So they brought it down to seven days, and then they brought it down to five days, and then down to three days. Now we've got it down to three doses. If you treat somebody with three doses today, in 1985, we know that that's as effective as three days, which is as effective as five or seven or ten days. So there is no reason to continue the antibiotics for any prolonged period of time."

"Over what period of time does it take to give three doses after the operation?"

"Usually twenty-four hours."

"So today, with this patient, even with a cut ureter, you would give her antibiotics for twenty-four hours."

"That's what I would do."

"And then stop them?"

"Yes, sir."

"In 1981 what was the thinking?"

"At that time the information about prophylaxis was not as clear. It was not down to the three doses that we know of today."

"Did you notice that Dr. Snider, in 1981, discontinued it after two days?"

"I have no problems with that."

"Was that good?"

"I have no problems with stopping the antibiotics."

"And is the state of the art in 1985 for prophylactic antibiotic therapy to be one day?"

"Yes, sir."

"And was it acceptable in 1981 to do it for two days?"

"Yes, sir."

Without another word Charlie walked to his chair and sat down, allowing the jury a few moments to grasp the significance of Dr. Orr's answers. Hogan had no further questions so the judge called for the next witness.

"We rest, your honor," said Tommy.

I wanted to rest, but could not. After a break for lunch we were to come back for Hogan's closing argument.

Chapter 25

> *'Tis not my talent to conceal my thoughts,*
> *or carry smiles and sunshine in my face,*
> *when discontent sits heavy at my heart.*
> —Addison

*I*n the summer of 1968 one could almost feel the tension in the air in Baltimore, Maryland. The broken windows, burned buildings, and abandoned row houses bore mute testimony to the racial riots that had ripped the ghettos a few months earlier. The June assassination of Robert Kennedy had seemingly taken away a glimmer of hope from the many impoverished victims of the slums who looked to him as a possible source of deliverance from their plight. The summer was hot and humid. Unemployment was high. Discontent festered, ever threatening to erupt again into full scale violence against the establishment. As is so often the case, though, the victims of deprivation vented their latent hostility on each other more frequently than on the perceived enemy.

Johns Hopkins Hospital stood in the midst of a veritable battleground, receiving almost nightly a steady stream of the city's youth — young gladiators, maimed by the guns and knives of their "friends." It was here I came as an intern that summer, fresh out of medical school to learn, among other things, how to care for victims of trauma. I spent the month of July in the emergency room before rotating in August to the male charity service where the majority of the trauma victims were operated upon and cared for.

In the late eighteen hundreds, the first professor of surgery at Johns Hopkins Hospital, William Halsted, had established the residency training program for surgeons. One of the principles that Dr. Halsted held most dear was that the surgical interns and residents should be on call twenty-four hours a day, seven days a week, a tradition that was maintained inviolate by his posterity. My days that August would begin at five each morning drawing blood for laboratory analysis on my patients before the resident arrived at six for rounds. It would usually be after midnight before I would stagger to my apartment across the street, weary from a day of assisting in surgery, performing history and physical examinations, changing dressings, caring for wounds, etc. As often as not, shortly after falling exhausted into bed, I would be awakened by a summons to return to the hospital to assist with an operation on another victim of the ongoing violence. It was not unusual to go for days with only a few snatches of sleep here and there. I was usually so fatigued that I could crawl onto an empty stretcher in the recovery room between surgical cases and be asleep within minutes. There were days when I felt as if I simply could not keep going if I did not get some rest.

A remarkably similar feeling overtook me Thursday afternoon as Hogan began his closing remarks. My fatigue was becoming so burdensome, I longed to be able to just put my head down and rest.

"Our burden of proof," said Hogan, "is to reasonably satisfy you that our side of the case is more likely true than their side. This case is not about the first surgery. This case is not about the fact that these doctors are qualified doctors. They are. This case is about two things — negligently severing a ureter, and the negligent follow-up care of that repaired ureter. That's all this case is about.

"In our society," he continued, "and I suppose this is true of other societies, too, the strong dominate the weak. In a court of law it's supposed to be different. The law puts everybody on an equal plane and says they start out even. I'm not blind, and I've been around a little while, and there is just no way in the world that I don't realize that in the social order of things maybe my client is not viewed in the same way as the defendants. That puts more pressure on you to start out even, and it won't be easy for you to do that. You are going to hear the judge tell you that a verdict is not supposed to be based on sympathy. You may think it means sympathy just in the case for the plaintiff and her injuries, but there are other kinds of sympathy. There is sympathy for the fact that there may be a lot of people in the courtroom, or people coming in here to sit down and create an aura. There may even be some occasion that would happen in a trial where children might run up and kiss one of the people involved in the trial and create sympathy. Things like that happen. Sometimes they don't happen by accident. Sometimes children are taken out of school and used in the courtroom."

Hogan was obviously not referring to the fact that Kathy's children had come to a part of the trial, though they had. He was referring to my eleven and thirteen-year-old sons, Jeff and Carey, who had also visited the trial briefly. Their school year had not yet started, so his implication that they had been taken out of school was erroneous. They had both leaned over and kissed me as they were leaving the court-room — something that is second nature to them. They al-ways kiss me when they leave, and have for as long as I can remember. If Hogan had implied earlier in the week that this had been staged, I would have been furious; but even my capacity to become angry was drained. His innuendos were making me more fatigued than angry. I just didn't want to hear any more. The effects of a week of fasting and insomnia had caught up with me. I slouched back in my chair, closed my eyes and rested my head in my hand. It was not the way I had been coached to sit during the week. I was supposed to be sitting up, attentive and somber, but I didn't care.

"It is no contest that these doctors know this procedure and are competent. There is no question in this case about the first surgery or that the cancer was removed or that cancer patients are entitled to the same quality of medical care as other patients. I am going to stop on that third one because it's very important. They say if he hadn't operated on you for cancer you would have died. The inference from that is, if you had died from cancer then nothing else ought to be important. So, I suppose that any surgeon who oper-ates on cancer can say in a case involving him, 'Well, if I didn't operate on your cancer, you would have died.' If it happens to be a case where the cancer was removed and, so far, the person is still alive, nothing else ought to matter. But the only place that leads is that cancer patients aren't as important as other patients. If nothing else matters, you can operate on a patient and negligently cost them a leg or other problem and it doesn't matter. Are we going to say that cancer patients don't matter? If we do, it certainly is a dangerous thing for us to do because there are lots of folks who get cancer. If what we do in our verdict is to essentially say that, even if there was negligence, even if the plaintiff proves his case, we are going to just say it doesn't matter because there was cancer and that was taken out, then that sure does give a lot of − well, it's a release in advance for anything anybody in that kind of work does. Well, that's not what the law is.

"Post-operative care is just as important as surgery," continued Hogan, reading from his poster. "The focus of the defense has, in every instance, been trying to get it back to that surgery − get your mind off the postoperative care. You know the only ones who have showed you the medical records in this case, as far as about the postoperative care, were us. Now let's talk about the negligence. I don't know what they're going to say now. I don't know whether they are going to say that the ureter was cut at the brim of the pelvis or that it was cut down deep inside. I don't know what their position is. Dr. Cameron seemed to say as he was called back to the stand the second time, it was cut down lower. I suspect that the reason that position was taken − clearly different from what the operative note says, even as their witness, Dr. Orr says − is that it is clear − Dr. Cameron admitted it − if the ureter was cut at the brim of the pelvis, that wasn't necessary. Didn't he say that? He did. And he said that if you carelessly cut a ureter after dissecting it out, just like the operative note says, that's negligence. So, if the ureter was cut at the brim of the pelvis in this operation, we have the defendant, together with the other evidence, admitting that it was negligence.

"But that's not really where the story ends. That's where it begins. Dr. Cameron, because of his personal situation, had a big responsibility with Kathy that he was having to trust to his partner, Dr. Snider. Now I want to talk about Dr. Snider's role in this case. No question that Dr. Snider is a very bright man and has plenty of training, and is competent to be what he is — a surgeon. He was plenty competent and was right there when the ureter was cut. He was plenty competent to take over and properly handle Kathy's case — if he just would have."

Dr. Cameron, aware that I was slumping in my chair, leaned over and told me to sit up. I had been worrying all week about what the jurors were thinking about my behavior. I had tried to do all the things that a "good defendant" is supposed to do, but I was tired of it. I was tired of Tommy telling me what to do. I was tired of Charlie telling me what to do, and I was tired of Dr. Cameron telling me what to do. I just didn't care anymore. If the jurors were going to convict me for being human and being exhausted, so be it. I ignored Dr. Cameron's admonition and continued to slump.

"Now, let's talk about what happened," continued Hogan. "Dr. Cameron sews the ureter back together, and the next day checks on Kathy and then leaves. He is gone! Doesn't reappear in the chart until the 5th or 6th of May. Kathy, as you will see from the temperature charts, starts a temperature. It's above a hundred almost constantly, certainly above normal almost constantly. Not only that, but going up and down — "spiking", as Dr. Lans says. The ureter, which has been cut and repaired is leaking. You see, you are going to have some drainage coming out of the Jackson-Pratt from the swelling — that clear, serous fluid. But Orr didn't talk about urine in large quantities coming out of there. That's what your record is going to show was happening here. Now, look at this. Here is something that is sewn together and leaking urine, and we have some temperature. Not only that, we went through those nurses' notes and, right there toward the end — pain! Crying with pain! Asking for the head nurse. Incredible pain! Then the temperature finally gets up to a hundred and one point something. 'What's that, Dr. Snider?' 'Well, that's the early evidence of the thrombophlebitis,'" said Hogan, mocking me. "Finally, on the 8th of May, we have the pain in the leg which is where the thrombophlebitis ended up being. We traced the clot, later in the records you will see, directly to that location where the ureter was cut — the pelvic brim. And we know from the chart, despite what the doctors say, the chart had sepsis all over it. Sepsis causes emboli. This infection which was there caused clots at the very location where the ureter had been repaired and which cost her, eventually, her leg.

"Afterwards, once the clots had formed, the doctors did a lot of things which were unavoidable, but by that time it was too late. The whole point is, by that time the chain of events had been set in motion by that early lack of attention. On the 15th it was all they could do to save her life. Finally, on the 15th, Dr. Cameron ordered a culture of that Jackson-Pratt drain. And what did it show? Incredible infection! I mean, my goodness! She was missing a whole section of her colon, and all this bacteria dumping into her body — and no antibiotics, and no cultures! Finally, on the 15th when she is almost dead, somebody gets around to taking a culture of the Jackson-Pratt drain. Twenty-three days after the drain was first put in somebody gets around to taking a culture, and the lady is almost dead. Finally, they prescribe a whole host of antibiotics and, thank goodness, her life was saved. It cost her the stroke and the leg.

"She is here after having lost a leg and a stroke. Why? Because there was no effort here to take the culture to see what was going on with the patient, despite the fact they knew that there would be bacteria in there. You say all this business about people ordinarily have bacteria, but people ordinarily don't have bacteria from their colon spilling into them which is going to happen after surgery like this.

"Dr. Snider was there at the surgery. Dr. Snider was bound to know the situation going on with Dr. Cameron at home. Dr. Snider knows more, by far, than anybody else in his firm and is watching the patient there for a week. Just as things start to go bad, on May 1st, the time when the patient is in there screaming with pain, crying, calling for the nurses, temperature is going up, antibiotics cut off — Dr. Snider jumps ship and doesn't reappear, in the chart at least, until the 23rd of May. After they have managed to save Kathy's life, and after she is just about to lose her leg, that's when you see Snider's name again. Is that reasonable? Is it reasonable for Dr. Snider to go off and do whatever he was going to do on that weekend and turn his patient over to somebody else in his office who had never seen her — didn't know anything about her? Is it reasonable for Dr. Snider to leave a little note for Dr. Morrow to consult? Nobody from John Cameron or Snider's service even there. Morrow decides on his own, without even being asked, to take a culture. When he did, what did he find? It was infection, and he prescribed an antibiotic. He hasn't been asked to take over this case. He is edging in because, obviously, the patient needs some help. So we say the doctors are negligent."

Even after listening to it for four days, I could still hardly believe the extent to which Hogan was distorting things and misleading the jury. I wondered if it bothered his conscience at all to be deliberately portraying us as being so wantonly negligent. Surely, I thought, there must be a better way — a system in which it is not necessary to make distorted personal attacks on others in order to win money for your client and yourself. It all seemed so unnecessary — so totally devoid of integrity.

In the final analysis, it would boil down to how much the jury believed the distortions and innuendos, and not to an educated study of the facts of the case in order to arrive at the truth. And this poor one-legged girl might become wealthy, or might leave with nothing, depending upon the whim of this particular jury. Another time, another place, a different jury might find just the opposite if given the same set of circumstances.

Hogan wrapped up his closing argument by suggesting to the jury how they could arrive at a proper award for his client. If I followed his reasoning, he seemed to be suggesting something in the order of a hundred dollars a day for the rest of her life. Assuming Hogan's fee to be the usual thirty to fifty percent of the award, he might receive as much as several hundred thousand dollars if the jury agreed with him — not a paltry sum for one who had been on the case for a few short weeks.

Chapter 26

Thursday Afternoon, August 29, 1985

An orator's virtue is to speak the truth.
—Plato

*C*harlie walked to the area in front of the jury box, legal pad in hand, to begin our closing argument. He appeared comfortable, even relaxed, as he began speaking to the jury. He had done it so many times before, he seemed to have a knack for knowing just what to say.

"Judge Price, ladies and gentlemen. I want to talk with you a little bit about these two doctors and about this case.

In listening to Mr. Hogan just then, I had the feeling that he
was admitting to all of us that Dr. John Cameron exercised
good care here, and that he really doesn't belong in this
case, because he said very little about him. He talked mainly
about postoperative care.   But I want to say this about
John Cameron.   For thirty-six years he has been here taking
care of us.   For thirty-six years he has given good service —
great service — to the citizens of his community.   He has
taken care of the poor people in the Tumor Clinic, as you
heard about.   He has taken care of the rest of us.   He took
care of Kathy Roberts when she needed him.   That's the kind
of man John Cameron has been.   He has taken care of the
people who need him the most.

"But after thirty-six years, he now finds himself in a court
of law, being brought here to answer and to explain about
his care for this patient — what he did — how he did it —
when he did it."   Charlie pointed to Hogan and said, "And
he asks you not to think about the result he got, that is,
saving her life. He says don't think about that. The case is
not about that.   But Dr. Cameron has been brought in here,
second guessed, criticized, with a suggestion that he didn't
tell you the truth — all of those things after the kind of life
and service he has given us.

"John Cameron answered the call, just as he always does,
when this patient was on that operating table, opened wide
up, and a bad, bad cancer was found.   I think that's one
thing everybody can agree on.   It was a bad, bad cancer.
A cancer in that area of her body is so much worse than a
cancer in other areas of the body.   And this cancer had
eaten all the way through the colon.   It had perforated
through and had spilled out, and the seeds of that cancer
were planted around her pelvic area.   On top of that, she
had a big abscess, an infection, a pool of pus.   She was in a
bad, desperate way.   She hadn't been prepared for major

surgery. It was a surprise, and they called for help to the best man that they had, the best man in this part of the state, one of the best men anywhere. He came, and he did his very best for her. He gave her all of his skill, and he cured that infection.

"They talk about not dealing with infection right — not knowing how to deal with it. He cured that one. He took care of that big pool of pus and that big abscess and that infection that was there. He took care of it completely, and he took that cancer out, and he saved her life.

"He followed her in the office, found that there was recurrence, and went back in for this major surgery. Now, she had to have that. There is no doubt about it. It was her only chance, and it's without dispute that going into that second operation her chances of dying in the operation were about ten percent. If you had ten women in exactly the same condition, one of them is going to die from the operation — at the University of Alabama, the University of Pittsburgh, anywhere. And these two fine doctors got her through that operation. She didn't die from the operation because of their skill and care. She had only a ten to fifteen percent chance to get through all of it without the cancer taking her life, and she's come through it. She's one of those ten or fifteen percent. The cancer is cured, as much as we can ever know. Coming up on five years now, and she is cured.

"But instead of a triumph, it's been called malpractice. Dr. Cameron has had to come here to defend himself, and Dr. Snider has had to come here and answer charges.

"To cure the cancer they had to cut all around the cancer and all these adhesions and scar tissue that had been formed by that previous problem. You heard Dr. Orr describe how you have to come all the way around and cut it all out if you are going to save her from cancer. If you are going to save her from cancer, you have to take healthy tissue along with the bad tissue. You've got to cut it. And that's what everybody wanted. That's what all of us would want. It had to be done. And when you take this much tissue, you are going to have complications, major ones, such that ten percent of the people die just from the operation."

Charlie put his hand on the rail in front of the jury box and leaned over, looking directly into the eyes of the jurors.

"But wouldn't we take that chance? Wouldn't we take that chance, that ten percent chance, because without it, it's a hundred percent? I think we would. And she did. And Dr. Cameron and Dr. Snider were willing to try to give her that chance.

"Now, I guess one way to avoid having complications in your operations is to do surgery that's minor, or surgery that doesn't carry with it many complications, or surgery that's easy. That would be one way. But if you are going to try to help people with this kind of surgery, then you are going to have complications. The University of Alabama has them. The University of Virginia has them. Everybody has them, and they had them, too — major complications with major surgery.

"I suppose the way to stay out of the courtroom and to keep from being sued is to take only easy cases and walk away from the hard cases and the people who are really in trouble and need you the most. Now that's not the kind of men these are. That's not the kind of man John Cameron is. He was willing. I wonder, though, if lesser men and lesser surgeons, if they know that this is what's going to happen to them, are going to be just as ready to step up and do their best without worrying about who is looking over their shoulder, and who is going to second guess them, and who is going to criticize them and blame them when the major complications come along."

I knew Charlie's words were sincere and not a scare tactic. He had been with so many physicians during times like this, and he knew how they felt. He knew many had already curtailed and limited their practices because of the fear of being sued. He knew others who had retired completely as a result of a lawsuit.

"So, they took this tissue, and in the process a ureter was cut. Mr. Hogan said in his opening statement, 'They dissected the ureter all the way down, looked at it all the way down, saw it, and still picked it up and cut it.' Now, if you believe that ———. The ureter was cut because, as the operative note says, 'everything in the pelvis was bound down with multiple adhesions from the previous surgery.' That's *everything* in the pelvis, including that part of the ureter. And all of them said, including Lans from Chicago, the gentleman who retired in 1979 and hadn't done a big operation since 1976, even Lans said if it's bound down in that scar tissue you can't see it. You can't tell it's there, so it's understandable and excusable if it's cut. That's what he said. That's why it was cut.

"Was there scar tissue at the point where it was cut? Well, this operative note says everything in the pelvis — *everything* in the pelvis — was bound down by multiple adhesions from the previous surgery. When they take anything out during surgery, it goes down to the lab and they look at it under a microscope. They really check it out, take their time, check it to find out just what it is and to make sure that everything was taken that should be taken. And here's what they said from the laboratory back on April 23, 1981. 'This entire area (the pelvis) is a mass of adhesions.' Were there adhesions and scar tissue in there?

The report of the operation says it. The laboratory study says it — the entire area, a mass of adhesions.

"Dr. Orr said everything is obliterated. You can't tell what's in there. You have to cut around it. You have to take it out, and if a ureter is in there, then that ureter just has to go, because this has got to come out. And they all cut them under this situation. Dr. Orr cuts them. Dr. Maddox cuts them. It happens to the best, because the best are in there trying to cure cancer, and they have to take tissue if they are going to cure cancer.

"Now it was repaired. It was repaired properly. Everybody says so. They had this drain, and you heard Dr. Orr say that at the University of Alabama Hospital they don't culture the drains because they've found out it's meaningless. They don't culture them. Are they wrong too? Are they all wrong? Is nobody right except the retired gentleman from Chicago and the Birmingham lawyer? Are they wrong not to culture drains? Don't you think they know how to deal with these things? And doesn't Dr. Cameron know, and Dr. Snider? They did so many things right. Would they just ignore that and forget about it and see that drain and walk away from it if it should be cultured? Did they forget about it? What does he say," said Charlie, motioning again toward Hogan. "He says they just forgot it, I guess — just didn't bother. Look at this medical record and see all of the tests and studies that they did on this lady, trying to help her. Would they just walk away from that if it should be cultured? They didn't culture it because that doesn't help. That's meaningless.

"They talk about cutting off the antibiotics. Mr. Hogan didn't mention that in his argument, but when he started this case that was a big part of what he was saying — that Dr. Snider just came by and discontinued the antibiotics —

willy-nilly discontinued it and that was careless. I think he knows now why it was discontinued and that it should have been discontinued. There was a good reason to discontinue it. You give antibiotics before the operation. You continue them a short time after the operation and then you cut it off, because if you keep it going continuously, you are going to cause problems, not solve them. If this happened today at the University Medical Center you would get antibiotics, three doses after the operation, twenty-four hours, and then it would be cut off whether a ureter has been cut or not. Four years ago they kept them going a little longer — two days. That's what Dr. Snider did. They used to keep them going longer until they realized what they were doing. They were causing problems with a superinfection. So modern medicine has realized that you have to cut back, not keep it going as long. Two or three days, four or five years ago. One day today. Dr. Snider did it exactly right — *exactly* right. Not negligent, careless. Not malpractice. He did it right and for a reason.

"Does it matter whether the ureter was cut at the pelvic brim or down closer to the bladder? The x-ray report, and you will see it, pretty well says where it was — just above the bladder, where the cancer was. But what if it was cut at the pelvic brim? Would that change anything? Would that matter? The pelvic brim is part of the pelvis, and it was part of the operation. That's where the adhesions were. The adhesions, you will remember, were in the entire area. As the pathology people said, or as Dr. Cameron wrote at the time, everything was bound down, including the pelvic brim. It doesn't matter whether it was the pelvic brim or just below that as it went into the bladder.

"Dr. Snider has not been doing this as long as Dr. Cameron. He has good training — University of Alabama Medical

School, Johns Hopkins Hospital. He is with the best group. He knows what he is doing. It was a tough situation and he, like Dr. Cameron, was willing to take it on. He did a good job with his management, and he deserves better than this.

"Just shortly it will be in your hands. All of the lawyers and the witnesses and the court will be through and it will be up to you. Dr. Snider and what he did will be judged by you. Dr. Cameron, after thirty-six years of service, will be judged by you. Some people might say it ought to be a medical school or a board of doctors — somebody who deals with this kind of thing to judge it. It may seem like that. But I think it's best that it's in your hands because, after all, the citizens of Montgomery ought to be the ones to judge them, and they are represented by each of you. I think it's fitting that it is in your hands and up to you to say what you will to John Cameron and to Howard Snider."

I wasn't sure at the time that I agreed with Charlie that the jurors were the best people to judge the case. With the passage of time I have become more convinced that I disagree with that position. The current system, however, is a boon to both the plaintiffs' and the defendants' attorneys. For every dollar paid in malpractice insurance premiums, the patients receive only twenty-eight cents. The remainder is eaten up by attorneys' fees, court costs, expert witnesses like Dr. Lans, etc. Somehow, the system needs to be changed such that a higher percentage of the money ends up in the hands of the injured.

Charlie sat down and Tommy walked to the jury box to give his part of our closing argument.

"Ladies and gentlemen of the jury, I appreciate, on behalf of Dr. Cameron and Dr. Snider, the efforts and the attention that you have given to hear this evidence — to learn this case. You know, we lawyers have been living this case for a while. We have been through these records and tried to interpret them the best we can. And then you are given four days. It's not an easy job. We recognize that, and we appreciate it very much.

"I would like to mention a little bit about the law, though, because the judge is going to charge you on the law. Mr. Hogan has stated that a plaintiff in a civil case just has to reasonably satisfy the jury that the plaintiff is right. Every citizen has the right to bring a lawsuit, but we have to give the defendant some protection that a plaintiff isn't going to bring a lawsuit that doesn't have merit. So what the law does is put the burden of proof on that plaintiff to reasonably satisfy you, by a preponderance of the evidence — to convince you — that not just one thing they say is true, but all of what they say is true.

"The law recognizes that doctors can't guarantee a cure. The law says that. The law recognizes the human nature of this situation. What must the doctor do? Well, a doctor must use reasonable care under the circumstances presented. First look at 'under the circumstances presented.' We've had a pretty good picture of that in this lawsuit. Circumstances change with each case. That's why, when Mr. Hogan states this case is not about one, two, three, four, he's wrong.

"Mr. Hogan said that if one party or another lies, they don't deserve to win. Well, I guess as soon as you get old enough to know what a lie is, those are kind of fighting words. That's a pretty harsh sounding thing and gets people upset. If you are lying you don't deserve anything, I guess. He and I may have a marked difference of opinion about the law, and I don't think it means that he's lying or that I'm lying. He said something in his opening statement that he was going to prove. He said this emboli shot up her leg into her brain. I've got it in the record. There is not one witness that took that stand and told you that a clot shot up her leg into her brain. In fact, he asked Dr. Lans — and I have that — the court reporter took it down, and it comes in the record. He asked what Dr. Lans thought were violations of the standard that, with a reasonable degree of medical probability, led to the loss of her leg and the stroke. Well, the answer was long, but he never said the stroke was related to anything that he criticized. Mr. Hogan asked him, and I am sure in the opening statement he thought he would say that, or he wouldn't have told you that. But I am not going to say that he was lying about it. That would be too harsh. He just couldn't prove it. That was a material part of their case that even their witness didn't support. You can't take what lawyers say at face value. You have to listen to the witnesses. It's crucial.

"You were told in closing statement that on May 1st, Dr. Snider, while this patient was screaming in pain, bailed out and left. You were told that Dr. Cameron does not appear in the record until May 4th or 5th. You see how thick the record is. I can show you in the record where Dr. Cameron, in the nurses' notes, was back on May 1st.

"You were told that they were the only ones that showed you the records. Well, they go first. Do you think that I am going to get up here after we have been through those records for two days and then say, 'Okay, doctor, take the stand and let's go back through those records one more time?' No. I would be a fool. You have seen them. I would bore you to death.

"Mr. Hogan has talked about Dr. Morrow, and he has presented it to you as if Dr. Morrow would have done something different — he would have cultured. What I can't figure out is why they keep ignoring — the Chicago lawyers heard it right before they got out of the case — and Dr.

Morrow said it again. Dr. Morrow, did that cut ureter have anything to do with thrombophlebitis? 'It had no relationship at all!''' mocked Tommy. "Dr. Morrow, did it have anything to do with that stroke? 'No.' Did Dr. Morrow suggest that a cut ureter means somebody was careless? He said, 'I repair them all the time.' Dr. Morrow came in on May 1st. The first thing he did was order a test, but it wasn't a culture. He didn't order a culture until May 4th — three days later. They are saying Dr. Snider jumped ship, and he had been doing something wrong. Dr. Morrow continued the same course! They are acting like Dr. Morrow would have made a difference. He told the Chicago crowd, he told them, and he told you — that cut ureter didn't cause any of that.

"Reasonable care is just that — what is reasonable under the circumstances. That's why we had to show you what these doctors faced.

"Now, if you find that Dr. Snider and Dr. Cameron acted reasonably, then you go no further. Your verdict is for the defendants. That's the end of your deliberations. Even if you find they didn't act reasonably, you must find that what they didn't do caused what she's suing for. We say they fail on both points.

"Back in 1981, Kathy Roberts' life did change. It wasn't fair. But life doesn't always deal with people the same way. At that time Kathy knew she would die without help, and at that time Kathy consented to major surgery. She placed no limits on Dr. Cameron. She said please get all the cancer out. But now that she's cured, she's forgotten that she accepted those risks. She's forgotten her consent. That's why we are here. When one undergoes this type of surgery — Dr. Lans even said it — one has to accept the risks. What is the ultimate risk? Death. She said I understood that, and I accepted it. But this was my chance. And she's been one of the lucky few who made it. And they say the case isn't about that.

"They tell you that Dr. John Cameron in this surgery exposed these ureters and carelessly cut one. They say, further, that he cut it where there was no cancer and no mass. That's what Dr. Lans tells you. Well, if there was no mass and no cancer and no adhesions there, what was he cutting? Have you asked yourself that? Dr. Lans didn't explain that. Really, what they are saying is Dr. Cameron just snipped it purposely. I don't think anybody would believe that about him. The record doesn't show that. The record shows the opposite. He cut it down where the cancer was — where the adhesions were — where Dr. Maddox and Dr. Orr said he had to assume there was cancer.

"Why would Dr. Lans say that? Why would he say that's the way it happened? Well, Dr. Lans, who retired in 1979, started doing this on the side, looking at records, working with these Chicago lawyers. He's experienced in cases. He knows what he has to say in order to say a doctor is negligent. But more importantly, he knows that it's unavoidable to cut a ureter in just the circumstances that Dr. Cameron and Dr. Snider and Patsy Paschenko described. He said it's unavoidable in circumstances when it's bound down. He admitted you can see it up top, and it can be bound down in the pelvis, and in that case it's not malpractice. So he knows he has got to say it occurred where it wasn't bound down. Then he knows he's got to say — because he has been in twenty or twenty-five lawsuits — he has to say that's what caused the problem. That's why he says that led to sepsis, which led to thrombophlebitis. He knows what he is doing in testifying.

"We bring two doctors from the University of Alabama,

as highly trained as anybody in the country, and they ask (motioning toward Hogan) 'Now, doctor, can you imagine what kind of pressure you would be under if you testified for the plaintiff?' What they are trying to tell you is that Dr. Morrow, Dr. Maddox, and Dr. Orr would come down here and tell you whatever is necessary to exonerate Dr. Cameron and Dr. Snider. They are trying to tell you that when they swore to tell the truth, under oath, that they then violated that oath and didn't do that.

"Well, I am going to say to you pressure is not coming to court and giving an opinion. Pressure is being down inside a lady's abdomen and pelvis, knowing you are the only thing that stands between her and death. I want to tell you that when they suggest that Dr. Cameron was careless when he snipped that ureter, that he was in there for three and a half or four hours standing between Kathy Roberts and death. That's pressure. Pressure is being called out at midnight with somebody who has been run over by a car and having to respond to the call. Pressure was being called in when she was wide open on the table with cancer eating through her bowel and abscessed. To suggest that some kind of pressure is going to make these people come in and tell you something other than the truth is so elementary that I cannot understand it. To suggest that these doctors, who have had the perseverance to go to school for twelve or thirteen years after high school to prepare themselves to come out and help their fellow man, will then, when they walk into a courtroom, turn into co-conspirators is something that I will never understand."

Tommy was putting himself into the argument like a Baptist preacher at a revival, possessed with a fervor to convince his listeners that his message was true and righteous.

He had been building up to a climax and, like an evangelist, turned to a human interest event that tugs at the heart-strings.

"You know, a few years back, a man jumped into an icy river and saved somebody drowning, and he immediately became a national hero. He was given a medal by the President. When John Cameron answered the call of a dying girl, and Dr. Snider helped him, they were sued. And they got a retired doctor from Chicago to spend a week or two going through these pages of records and, after all of that, he comes up with two things. Don't let a suggestion of pressure fool you. They know what pressure is, and they know how to handle it. We are lucky in this community that they are here and they will be here to handle it. We are lucky. You can't find better trained, more competent doctors."

I don't know what effect Tommy was having on the jury, but he was playing havoc with my fragile emotional state. I had been sitting there all week, with some people implying that I was a callous villain and others that I was a hero. In truth I was neither — only a man who tries his level best to care for others as he would want to be cared for. But I could contain the emotions no more. Tears began to trickle down my cheeks as Tommy began wrapping up his closing argument.

"John Cameron and Howard Snider could have easily said this is big, bad, risky surgery. You can die from it. You can get thrombophlebitis from it. You can have a stroke. You may lose a leg. You may lose both legs. I would rather not do it. They could have done that, but they gave her that chance. She could have said I'd rather not have all this done, but she took what they offered — her only hope. And they beat it. They beat insurmountable odds fighting with her and for her.

"A verdict in any amount will tell these doctors they were careless — they were reckless. I don't care how simple they try to make it, this verdict will be your public pronouncement. I know these men, and I'm proud to know them. I ask you to applaud them, to encourage them to take the risk in the future. I ask you not to give a negative vote for medical care by telling doctors that, if you take a big, risky case, and you have what everybody has as a complication, we're going to get you. If you don't think this is important to these men who have devoted their whole lives to come out in the middle of the night while others sleep, to save people, then you have missed the whole point of our case. I am sorry if that has happened, because I haven't done my job. They fought for Kathy every step of the way. They didn't abandon her. They didn't turn away from her. Please don't tell them, after that, that they were negligent — that they committed medical malpractice. Please don't tell Dr. Maddox and Dr. Orr, who do these procedures too, that anytime you have these complications that you tell us that you are going to have, you are going to be called in. That would set us back a hundred years. If we're not willing to take risks, we're never going to effect cures.

"We never know why some people are dealt the unfair blow of cancer, but we better hope we continue to have people courageous enough to undertake to cure it. Not many are called upon in society to save a life. Not many are able. Please don't discourage those who are and who are willing to. I ask you to give your public thanks to these doctors for saving not only Kathy's life, but the many others they have and will. There is but one way to do it. That's a verdict for the defendants. Thank you very much."

I had a strange sense that for Hogan to speak at that moment would be inappropriate — almost irreverent. I

longed for that to be the end of the arguments — to let
the trial end on that note, but it was not to be. As tears
continued to trickle from my eyes, Hogan rose once again
to have the final words.

"The new element that's now introduced into this case
by these arguments is the element of sympathy called fear.
I'm going to call it what it is, folks. This is just nothing
but a threat. Haven't you just heard something like this?
No matter what the facts are, if you return a verdict in
this case in favor of the plaintiff, somehow doctors will be
afraid to do surgery? Isn't that just an appeal to your fears?
That's exactly what it is, and you know it. These people
who just said that know it. You can't judge facts fairly
if you are laden down with all kinds of fears and sympathies
for people. Lawyers who make arguments based on sympathy, who appeal to the sympathies of a jury, are not
doing a service to the job you jurors have to do back there
in that jury room. It's hard enough as it is to sit down
and look at facts. It's not easy to prove a doctor guilty
of negligence.   The   law   didn't   make   it   easy."

I agreed with Hogan that, to an extent, the arguments
had appealed to the jurors' emotions and sympathies. But
so had his. Both sides recognized the importance of that.
The system made that approach almost mandatory if one
hoped to win. There was no way the jurors were equipped
to make the decision based on an analysis of the facts. We
knew before the trial began that we didn't have a chance
at really getting them to understand the details of the case.
Their decision would be based upon a partial, somewhat
confused knowledge of the facts, coupled with their opinion of us as people — how we behaved, how we dressed,
and how we looked. We knew that their emotions would
be at least as important as their intellects in reaching a

decision. For the system to be that way is dead wrong.

Hogan pointed toward our attorneys and said, "He said we haven't proven infection. Now, we had a lots of folks up here expressing opinions, but we finally got one of them, not even a witness for us, a witness for them — one book finally made it in as being an authority, a standard. The standard says if you have a catheter in, you ought to be giving antibiotics. Their witness said it was a standard.

"They say we don't have any proof about stroke. The record proves the stroke. Septic emboli, septic infarct is the word that's used in the record. That's what she had. I don't really remember now whether that was even included in Dr. Cameron's summary, but I think something about septic was in his discharge summary.

"The Chicago crowd. Okay, the Chicago crowd — the Chicago lawyers. I'm an Alabama lawyer. I'm in this case and the reason I'm in this case is because it's a good case. Kathy Roberts deserves good representation, and without it she wouldn't have a chance. I don't know if I have done a good job, and I'm afraid I haven't. I know what I'm up against, but I'm trying.

"Here is the question, folks. You go in for surgery. You have to sign a piece of paper. You have to say I understand I might die. It's one of the risks of surgery. Let's just ask the question, does that mean a doctor doing surgery is free to do anything he wants to that patient — even kill them? Is he free to do anything he wants in surgery? Does he have any limitations at all?

"I don't care if Dr. Cameron has been in practice thirty-six years. That just shows he knew that much more about it. Dr. Cameron said you shouldn't cut this ureter at the pelvic brim. He said at another point that if you cut a ureter that had been clearly dissected and you cut it carelessly, that would be negligent. Now here we have the doctor admitting it. Now given the fact that he has admitted negligence, does that not count? Well, it doesn't if we are going to just say that doctors can do anything they want in surgery. And that's what they would like you to say. Don't be afraid to be honest. All we ask you to do is have the courage to tell the truth.

"Justice is a statue, and when we go to law school we see a little statue called justice, a woman wearing a blindfold, holding a scale. And you just blindfold yourself to the sympathies and fears and prejudices and you weigh the evidence. And your verdict, when all twelve of you can agree on something, speaks the truth. That's the system. It's been around for hundreds and hundreds of years. It traces back to ancient England. The number twelve came from the fact that there were twelve apostles. This is an old, old, old system. We trust it. Both sides of this case trust it. No, we don't have doctors judging this. We have people off the street who don't know either side. If you did, you wouldn't be on the jury. We have people who can be fair to both sides. If you couldn't, you wouldn't be on the jury.

"These doctors have been inconvenienced this week, and we apologize for that and their families. But they are through with this case when this week is over. Kathy is not. When I'm gone, as I'll be after this case, I may never see Kathy again, and you may never see Kathy again. But she will have to live with the results of this case. Now, if it is a true verdict, we will all be proud of it. But let it be based on the facts and the evidence. Thank you."

My tears had stopped. I was relieved that Hogan had now said all that he would and could. The feeling I had toward him at that moment was not unlike one I had felt in the distant past. To me, he was the neighborhood brat. I just wanted him to go away.

Chapter 27

Tears fall, no matter how we try to
check them, and by being shed
they ease the soul.
—Seneca

After a brief recess, Judge Price charged the jury on the points of the law applicable to this particular case, and on how the jurors were to go about the process of reaching a verdict. The judge read through his instructions to the jury so rapidly that I feared they would not be able to follow everything he was saying. Fortunately, he repeated most of the things at least a time or two. I was comforted somewhat by the knowledge that several of them were taking notes during the charge, and I hoped that they would get most of the important points through repetition.

Judge Price explained to the jurors that, since the plaintiff had brought the charges against us, she had the burden to prove to their reasonable satisfaction, by a preponderance of evidence, that what she contends is more likely true than not. He reiterated that this charge of malpractice basically boiled down to a charge that we were negligent.

"Negligence," he said, "is the failure to do what a reasonably prudent person would have done under the same or similar circumstances, or the doing of something which a reasonably prudent person would not have done under the same or similar circumstances. Now, the plaintiff is saying that, as a result of their not doing what a prudent, reasonable person would have done in this case that she suffered injuries, and their omission to perform to the standard is the proximate cause of her injuries. The law defines proximate cause as follows: the proximate cause of an injury is that cause which, in the natural and probable sequence of events and without the intervention of any new or independent cause, produces injury and, without which, such injury would not have occurred."

Judge Price then touched on an aspect of the law that has important implications, not so much for our case, but to all recipients of health care. It insures that citizens in Montgomery can expect their surgeon to keep abreast of the latest developments in surgery across the country and afford them the same quality care as a citizen of Boston, Chicago, New York, or any other city.

"The law says that, in performing a professional service for a patient, a physician must use that degree of care, skill, and diligence which is ordinarily possessed and used by physicians in the same general practice in the national community in the line of practice under similar circumstances," he said.

Were it not for this law, physicians in a given community could all practice an outdated, inferior brand of medicine, and it would not be malpractice, because it is the "standard" for the community. The down side to the law, however, is that it opens the door for professional "hired guns" to make their living by traveling to distant cities to testify against local physicians. The law does not impose any criteria upon such "hired guns" as far as their qualifications for being expert in a given field is concerned. They need only to have a degree in medicine and profess to be an expert in the particular field in question. Dr. Williams, the Sarasota physician who gave a deposition in our case was a general surgeon by training. In the past he had testified in a court case in Montgomery as an expert in neurology!

Judge Price informed the jury that Kathy was seeking compensatory damages for her pain and suffering, mental anguish, permanent disfigurement, and impairment of her ability to earn. He explained that, if they found in her favor, the law does not specify any guidelines as to the amount that they should award, but leaves that solely up to the discretion of the jury. The only stipulation imposed by the law is that, if damages are awarded, they must be reasonably supported by the evidence and cannot be based upon guess, speculation, or conjecture.

He then continued, "I charge you that a doctor is not an insurer of a successful result of his treatment. The law does not require that physicians such as Dr. Cameron and Dr. Snider should be perfect or infallible in their treatment of a patient. They are not liable for even an error in judgment where the proper course was pursued, or where the proper course is subject to reasonable doubt, provided they exercised the same degree of care, skill, and diligence as physicians in the same general national community and in the same general line of practice under the same or similar circumstances.   Dr. Cameron and Dr. Snider cannot be held liable for negligence in this case, or of malpractice in this case, merely because some other physician would have used a different approach.   The test is whether they used reasonable and ordinary care under the circumstances presented to them.   If there are various recognized methods of treatment, the doctor is free to choose the one he thinks best and is not liable for negligence because some expert witness gives the opinion that some other method would have been preferable.

"The rule in this malpractice suit is that there must be something more than a mere possibility, something more than one possibility among others, that the alleged negligence or malpractice complained of was the proximate cause of the plaintiff's injuries.   If the injury and damage claimed by the plaintiff would have occurred regardless of any act or omission by Dr. Cameron and Dr. Snider, then the act of omission was not the proximate cause of these injuries, and Dr. Cameron and Dr. Snider would be entitled to a verdict in their favor."

Judge Price told the jurors that they owe no obligation to either party.   They were to be seekers of the truth, sifting through the evidence to make it all come out and speak the truth, and to reach a verdict based upon the facts, regardless of any feelings that they may have of sympathy, prejudice, or passion.   They were to decide which witnesses to believe, whether or not the witnesses were in a position to know what they testified about, and whether or not they told the truth. Whatever verdict they reached was to be unanimous.

After completing the charge to the jury, Judge Price sent the twelve regular jurors to the jury room to begin their deliberations. It was fifteen minutes past three on Thursday afternoon. There was nothing to do now but wait. It was a feeling somewhat akin to that which comes upon completing a major final examination. After months of preparation and hours of participation, the job was finished. We had done our best. We could second guess how we could have prepared better or answered questions better, but nothing could be changed now. It was in someone else's hands now to determine our final grade.

We had hoped the jury would be out a short period of time and quickly return a verdict in our favor, but it was not to be. As time wore on and their deliberations continued, it became apparent that we had not convinced them we were right — at least not all of them. At that moment Hurricane *Elena* was hovering in the Gulf of Mexico off the coast of Alabama and Florida, first going one way then the other as if she were taunting the inhabitants along the coast, rather than quickly unleashing her fury and striking one or the other. It seemed to me that the jury and the hurricane were going to behave similarly.

My fatigue increased with each passing minute, until it became almost unbearable. Finally, just before six o'clock, Judge Price gave instructions to the jurors to decide whether they wanted to continue deliberating into the night, or recess and return again in the morning. A great conflict raged within me as they considered what they wanted to do. I desperately wanted to go to sleep exonerated that night. The anguish of not knowing was producing enormous anxiety, much like that which patients feel when they await the report of a biopsy. Even if the report is cancer, it is easier to cope with it once the diagnosis is known. I wanted to know if I were going to be found negligent so I could begin the process of coping, or I wanted to be taken off the hook. On the other hand, I did not believe I could physically or emotionally endure much more that night.

I also had the strangest feeling that seemed almost inappropriate, so much so that I dared not share it with anyone — even Pam. Win or lose, I did not think I could recover from the trauma of the week quickly enough to return to work the following morning. Yet I knew that I would feel terribly guilty if I took the day off just to rest. Our partners had been working hard that week doing their work as well as ours, and they too were tired. If the jury decided to continue deliberating the following morning, I could then go home and go to bed, and I would not have to worry about trying to face going to work again so soon. So fragile was I that I even wanted them to hurry up and decide what they were to do, so I wouldn't have to think about which way I would prefer. They were mercifully quick in deciding to recess for the evening. When we got home, I ate a quick supper, told Pam I didn't want to talk to anyone who might call, and went to bed at seven o'clock.

The newspapers that week had done a tolerable job of reporting the case up to that point. However, the following morning there was an article in *The Montgomery Advertiser* which exasperated me. It contained the following paragraph which was grossly misleading.

"Hogan told the jury that Ms. Roberts is suing not only because of the severed ureter, but because poor medical treatment she received after the operation caused the doctors' [sic] to not realize they had cut the ureter."

No one, not Dr. Lans, not even Hogan, had at anytime implied anything other than the fact that we had immediately recognized the injured ureter and appropriately repaired it. Yet, the newspaper was telling our friends, patients, and referring physicians that we were, in essence, so inept that we did not even realize we had cut the ureter. It seemed rather careless of the reporter to write that when it had never been an issue in the case. I suppose it was as difficult for him to follow the facts as it was for the jurors.

The jury reconvened at eight-thirty Friday morning to resume deliberations. Since we had to be present when they finally returned a verdict, we had to hang around the courtroom the entire time. There was nothing to do but wait, pace the floor, and agonize.

It was a little awkward with Kathy and her family also sitting there waiting just as anxiously, hoping for a different verdict. For her, the jury's decision probably meant the difference in her walking away with nothing, or with several hundred thousand dollars. For us, the difference was a little less tangible but equally as important. There were some things that were easy to identify as being harmful to us if the jury returned a verdict against us. Our malpractice insurance premiums would no doubt increase. We would receive the negative publicity in the newspaper, worse than we had already received, and our reputations would be further tarnished. There was the awful possibility that, if we continued to take care of high risk patients and had other judgments against us, our insurance carrier might be forced to drop our coverage altogether, making it impossible for us to practice anymore. But somehow these were not the major things that bothered me. The greatest impact would be upon me as an individual, quite apart from any monetary or societal consequences. To know for certain that I had carefully and conscientiously participated in

Kathy's care and, even in retrospect, could have made no changes in my management that would have altered her ultimate outcome, yet still be judged by a "jury of my peers" to be guilty of negligence and malpractice would be devastating.

Already I felt "violated" just by being charged with these offenses. So often in the past when I read in the newspapers of people being charged with various things, I assumed the likelihood was high that they had done something wrong; the trial was to determine whether this wrong could be proven. During the week of our trial I wondered if my friends and patients had made the same unfair assumption about me — that I had erred, and the plaintiff was trying to prove it. Just to have this doubt planted in people's minds was painful enough to me, but to have the jury acknowledge that my guilt had been "proven" would have been unbearable.

The wait seemed like an eternity but was actually only two and a half hours. Shortly before eleven we were notified that the jury had reached a verdict. As we took our seats there was a lump in my throat. My heart was pounding and my hands were trembling. As the jurors filed back into the jury box to take their seats, I searched their faces for clues. They would not look at us! I felt that they were deliberately avoiding eye contact with us. Even the smiling face on the back row that I had been certain about seemed to be avoiding me. Dr. Cameron obviously read them the same way I did. "Guilty," he muttered under his breath.

"Ms. Foreperson, has the jury reached a verdict?" asked the judge when all of the jurors were seated.

"Yes, sir, we have," she replied.

"Pass it up please."

The verdict form was passed up to Judge Price, who silently looked at it without showing any emotion. After a brief pause, he read it aloud.

"We, the jury, find in favor of the defendants, Dr. John Cameron and Dr. Howard Snider."

For a moment I sat there, Judge Price's words reverberating in my brain. I had feared that the long deliberation by the jury and their faces when they returned to the court room were harbingers portending ill will for us. I had to play the words back in my mind before I was really sure the verdict was in our favor.

Oh, what sweet words they were to my ears, bringing vindication and justice, after months and months of agony. I could contain myself no longer. Tears began to flow freely down my cheeks. No longer were they tears of anguish; they were tears of joy. We hugged, and we cried, and we sighed, and we celebrated. It was over. The long ordeal — the nightmare — had finally ended.

Chapter 28

One may smile, and smile, and
be a villain.
—Shakespeare

When our trial ended, I was unable to simply walk away from it and put it behind me. The exhilaration that I thought I should feel as the "winner" somehow eluded me. Rather than winning anything, I had, in fact, lost a great deal. I had spent a whole week away from my practice — just sitting in the courthouse most of the time. For weeks, even months, I had not had enough time to devote to my patients because I was busy preparing for the trial. I had been spending my spare time reading about a problem that had occurred four years earlier rather than reading about the problems my current patients were facing. The days of the trial and the preceding weeks of preparation had been both physically and emotionally exhausting. The whole ordeal had created so much emotional turmoil that it had pushed me to the very brink of my ability to cope. I dreaded the thought of ever having to go through another trial again and empathized with all of my fellow physicians who were experiencing the same agony.

My personal encounter with how our legal system works had left me disillusioned and dismayed. I wasn't sure exactly how the system should work, but one thing was crystal clear. I knew that medical malpractice cases should be removed from the jury system. Our inability to just explain the facts to someone who could understand them had been frustrating, to say the least. I felt strongly that a panel of inquisitive, highly educated people who could understand a rational presentation of the medical details would be far preferable to a jury of people who didn't have a ghost of a chance at following even an elementary synopsis.

I also resented the way our legal system encourages the plaintiffs' attorneys to portray the accused doctor as an incredibly careless, wantonly negligent reprobate. He *must* convince the jury that the doctor was negligent in order to recover damages for his client. Except for this legal requirement, it really makes little difference whether a person's injury results from a mistake caused by negligence or a mistake that results from just being human and, therefore, fallible. The line separating the two is so indistinct that it is frequently almost imperceptible; and the end result of the mistake is the same. To carry the reasoning one step further, it really makes little difference whether the injury results from a mistake or from an "act of God." The pain and suffering the victim must endure are the same. Currently, we compensate only those patients whose pain and suffering result from negligence. Is that the policy we wish to continue? Or do we want to compensate patients for all bad results caused by mistakes? Or even for all bad results? In any event, the decision as to what transpired in the case should be made by an educated evaluation of the medical details; and the amount of compensation should be determined by a rational, uniform assessment of the degree of impairment — not by the emotional whim of a jury.

During the days that followed our trial, my resentment for what I had been through, and my opinion that it had all been so unfair, would not go away. I felt that I could not be content until I had told my story, so I decided to write my first book. One of the first things I did was to contact many of the jurors and arrange for interviews while things were still fresh on their minds. I wanted to ascertain, among other things, how well they had followed the medical testimony during the week, and what their level of understanding was concerning what had actually happened to Kathy. I was afraid that they had been confused by the conflicting accounts they had heard and that they lacked the background to be able to sort out the truth. My suspicions were confirmed. Their knowledge of the medical events was, at best, sketchy. It was not because of a lack of intelligence. Some of the jurors were quite articulate, and several were well educated in fields other than science. It was simply unrealistic to expect people with no scientific background to follow even a simplified version of what happened, particularly when they had no opportunity to ask questions or clarify misunderstandings.

In talking with the jurors, I began to piece together what

had transpired behind the locked door of the jury room. I was shocked to find that the woman on the back row with the smiling face — the one who was clearly "on our side" — was one of our most adamant, outspoken critics. A divorcee, already struggling to care for four sons, she had adopted her nephew a few months earlier when his parents died within a few weeks of each other. Convinced that poor nursing care at Baptist Medical Center had contributed to her sister's death from diverticulitis, she harbored a deep-seated bitterness toward the medical profession in general, a bias which had gone unacknowledged in the *voir dire*. She betrayed herself when she told me she thought it was the hospital and not we who should have been sued. What had the hospital done to Kathy to deserve a lawsuit? And, if she truly felt that way, why did she vote against us? It seemed that the hospital bore the majority of her bitterness, but we were the scapegoats. It was as though she had a vendetta, and it would somehow help alleviate her sorrow if someone atoned for her lost sibling. I suppose, in retrospect, the smile from the back row which I had interpreted as meaning "I'm with you" in actual fact was conveying "I'm going to get you." So much for my training in counseling to be able to read people's faces.

Another juror, the Pizza Hut waitress, had also had a bad experience with the medical profession, a bias which was also unacknowledged in the *voir dire*. She was persistent in her efforts to persuade the other jurors that we should be found guilty of negligence. She had thought Dr. Cameron had been lying about the location of the cut ureter. Long after the other jurors had resolved that issue, she continued to bring it up. She was also convinced that Dr. Orr had been lying because he seemed fidgety in the chair. Her irrational, emotional arguments and her tendency to disagree with essentially everything, eventually became a source of annoyance to the other jurors.

The other dissenting votes came from three of the black jurors; the LPN who worked at a nursing home, the young navy recruiter, and the wife of a funeral home director. I had been skeptical of the common belief that defendants should avoid black jurors, if possible, because they most commonly side with the plaintiff. However, seventy-five percent of the black jurors had sided with Kathy, even though both the plaintiff and the defendants were white.

I was not in the least bit surprised at the LPN. There was just something in her manner which made me believe all along that she was going to oppose us. She believed that the cut ureter had caused infection which had, in turn, caused thrombophlebitis which had led to all of the other problems.

The wife of the funeral home director, originally an alternate, would not have even been on the jury had not the tire changer, who had years before voted for Tommy's defendant in a malpractice trial, misunderstood the judge's instructions and failed to show up for an afternoon session. His replacement was much harder on us than he likely would have been. At least, though, according to some of the jurors, she was more rational in her arguments than the other dissenters.

When the jurors were unable to reach a unanimous decision on Thursday night, they decided to recess and go over things in more detail on Friday. When they reconvened, they went through the chart, day by day, comparing progress notes, orders, nurses' notes, temperature sheets, etc. Only then were they able to see that Hogan's assertions just did not hold up under scrutiny. Ultimately, they all agreed, or at least acquiesced, and reached a unanimous verdict.

I was distressed to learn that perhaps the single thing that bothered the jurors the most was the fact that I had "jumped ship." When Hogan had made that allegation, we had thought it so ridiculous that we really didn't spend much time explaining that it wasn't so. It was bad enough that the jurors who were basically against us felt that way. However, one of the ones who had thought all along that no malpractice had been committed and who had been an advocate of ours in the jury room, also had reservations about that period of time. She wrote to me, "Dr. Morrow became the 'White Knight' because he assumed responsibility for Kathy's care while Dr. Cameron was in Europe and Dr. Snider had his weekend rotation off." Hogan had successfully portrayed to the jury that Dr. Morrow had been forced to step in because we were neglecting Kathy during that period of time. In actual fact, our partner, Dr. Ingalls, had assumed her care during that weekend, until Dr. Cameron returned on Monday. Dr. Morrow, while a good doctor, was no 'White Knight,' and he did not assume her care at any time. He did what any other good urologist consultant would have done, but *we* cared for her on a daily basis.

The juror further wrote, ". . . we all agreed that for those few days, it may not have been negligent care, but it was not the first quality care we would all want and expect." I was crushed when I read those words. Even she, one of my partner's patients, did not understand; or worse, perhaps she understood, and represents a societal expectation which is greater than we were able to satisfy. Her words referred to the weekend I was off and the days following it — the time, according to Hogan, when I had "jumped ship." I had been primarily responsible for Kathy during the week when Dr. Cameron was out of town. At that time, she was a routine surgical patient, recovering uneventfully from a major operation — not a young person with an amputation and a stroke. Dr. Cameron was back and had assumed her care again long before she became desperately ill. The jurors, knowing that two weeks later she was to be at death's door wanted me to somehow be clairvoyant and realize at the time what they knew in retrospect. Presumably, in their minds, had I known that she was to become ill, I would not have taken the weekend off, leaving Dr. Ingalls to care for her, but would have stayed by her bedside.

There are some major problems with the expectations implicit in the words of my partner's well-intentioned patient. I obviously cannot accurately predict which patients will develop complications and be likely to ultimately file suit against me. Even if I could, though, "first quality care" would still include taking time off and entrusting their care to someone else. Almost every weekend that I am off, I leave patients that I, not Dr. Cameron, have operated upon, who are sicker than Kathy was at that time. If I am to continue to take care of high risk patients on a regular basis, I must do it that way, or, literally, be on call all the time. Did the jurors really expect me to have no time off? Does the public expect me to work constantly, falling asleep on stretchers in the recovery room as I did when I was an intern? I shudder when I contemplate the quality of care I would deliver under such circumstances.

It is ironic, after listening to Hogan say all manner of evil against us during the trial, and hearing an account of some of the jurors' hostile comments about us, that I would be wounded most by the words of a well-intentioned sympathizer.

Chapter 29

Fall, 1985

"He means well" is useless
unless he does well.
—Plautus

We had just begun to relax and get back into our usual routines when we were notifed in early September that Hogan had filed a motion for a new trial, the alleged grounds being that the defense counsel had appealed to the sympathy, bias, and prejudice of the jury during closing statements, thereby denying the plaintiff a fair trial by an impartial jury. The

motion asserted that we had appealed to the passion, prejudice, and fear of the jury by arguing that a verdict against
the defendants would induce some surgeons to fear to
operate. In addition, since saving the patient's life was never
an issue in the trial, statements that the defendants had
saved the plaintiff's life were also said to be direct appeals
to passion, prejudice, and bias.

Several weeks later Hogan filed an amendment to his
motion, claiming that Judge Price had unfairly prejudiced
the case by ruling that Dr. Robert Pieroni, an internal medicine specialist in Tuscaloosa, could not be called as a witness. I had been intrigued back in February when Dr. Pieroni's name had appeared on the list of witnesses at the same
time as Dr. Williams'. I wondered if he also testified in malpractice trials for a living or advertised in *Trial* magazine.
He was from my hometown, not some distant location,
and I could not help wondering how he had become involved in the case.

Susan Loggans had represented to Judge Price in a pretrial
conference that Dr. Pieroni was to testify only against the
hospital and would offer no testimony against the physicians. The hospital's attorney, on numerous occasions,
requested Lee DeWald to make Dr. Pieroni available for
deposition, to no avail. When Hogan finally assumed responsibility for the case, he offered to make Dr. Pieroni
available to us, but it was past the cutoff time for depositions in the case. These circumstances precluded Dr. Pieroni from testifying during the trial.

My interest in Dr. Pieroni soared when I read an affidavit attached to the amended motion which was signed
several weeks after our trial had ended. In it he stated,
"It was and is my opinion that the sepsis condition that
developed in Kathy Roberts postoperatively was, with

reasonable medical probability, the cause of her loss of leg and her stroke. It was further my opinion that the sepsis condition was caused because of postoperative care that was deficient and that did not meet the minimum standard of care applicable to physicians in the state of Alabama."

It seemed incredible to me, if he had full knowledge of everything that had been presented at the trial, including her problem with *Heparin,* that he would still really believe that explanation. I suspected that he had only been given an abbreviated version of what had transpired at the trial and had, in essence, been duped. Again I wondered what was motivating him to involve himself in the case. Was he a man of principle who honestly wanted to do what was right and thought he was helping improve the quality of medical care in Alabama? If so, I thought he was severely misguided. Was he a "hired gun," willing to say anything in return for a fee? I knew when I read the affidavit that I eventually wanted to find out.

On October 21st, Judge Price issued an order denying Hogan's request for a new trial. Forty-two days later, after the time allowed by law for appeal to the Supreme Court had expired, we breathed the ultimate sigh of relief. Hogan had filed no further appeals, and we were forever removed from jeopardy in the Kathy Roberts case. One week later I made my first contact with Dr. Pieroni in the following letter:

December 9, 1985

Dr. Robert Pieroni
P. O. Box 6291
University, Alabama

Dear Dr. Pieroni:

On October 21, 1985, Judge Charles Price denied the motion for a new trial in Kathy Roberts' case. (The 42 days allowable under the law to file a notice of appeal expired on December 2nd. I have deliberately waited to contact you until no further action could be taken against us in the case, in order to avoid being construed as attempting to influence your opinion.

I am convinced that Kathy Roberts received not only the minimum standard of care applicable to physicians in the state of Alabama, but, in fact, received a very high level of care which is responsible, in part, for her being alive today. I have your affidavit of September 26, 1985, stating your opinion that her postoperative care was deficient and did not meet the minimum standard of care, and that she developed sepsis postoperatively which was, with reasonable medical probability, the cause of her loss of leg and her stroke. If I felt that you were a "hired gun", willing to say anything for money, I would not waste my time contacting you. However, because I believe in all probability you are sincere in your belief that we committed malpractice and, no doubt, feel that you were doing the right thing by offering to testify against us, I feel compelled to contact you and attempt to discuss the case with you.

Dr. Pieroni, please understand that I bear no malice toward you for your action. I do not subscribe to the belief that physicians should "stick together" in a conspiracy of silence and turn their heads when they see instances of malpractice.

I am in the process of writing a book about this ordeal, which for me has been a personal nightmare. In order to write it accurately, I need to better understand your thoughts about the case and your motivation for becoming involved. I believe if we could get together and go over the details of the case, it might be enlightening and beneficial to each of us.

I am planning to come to Tuscaloosa to visit with my parents right after Christmas and would like an opportunity to get together with you at your convenience. I can meet you anywhere, at any hour you select. My only request would be that it be at a time when we could spend between one and two hours together discussing the case in an unhurried manner. Please let me know if you are willing to do this and, if so, when it would be convenient for you so that I can arrange my schedule accordingly.

Sincerely,

Howard C. Snider, M.D.

I was pleasantly surprised to receive a cordial and encouraging reply from him a short time later. After complimenting me on the general tone of my letter (considering the circumstances), he wrote that he would be pleased to meet with me and discuss Kathy's case and other germane issues. He was even gracious enough to invite me to his home for a relaxed, unhurried visit during the holidays.

I was thrilled. Perhaps, I reasoned, he was the type of person who was concerned that physicians should be doing more to police their own ranks, and he was sincere in his belief that he had been doing the right thing. If so, I was certain some good would come from our meeting. Also, in a curious sort of way, a rational discussion of the hard evidence of the case with Dr. Pieroni was important to me in order to achieve final vindication and absolution. I was convinced that, if we looked at the facts together, he would almost surely reach the inescapable conclusion that Kathy's amputation and stroke resulted from an allergy to *Heparin*, not negligent care. I thought it most likely that an allergy to *Heparin* had not even occurred to him when he reviewed the chart.

When I called Dr. Pieroni, he again graciously invited me to meet with him in his home and consented to my request to be allowed to tape-record the interview. However, my elation was short-lived. Within a week, I received another letter.

Dr. Pieroni wrote that he had just learned about several aspects of Kathy's trial which caused him to believe that it would not be beneficial to anyone for us to discuss the events which led to the trial in this "unfortunate case". He wrote that he thought those aspects which he had recently learned should best remain private. After assuring me that he had acted in good faith and with a clear conscience, he wished me the best of luck.

What had he found out that had caused him to change his mind? Had he just now realized that *Heparin*, not sepsis, was the culprit, and he was now embarrassed to acknowledge that fact? Perhaps he had been misled by being given only partial information before signing the affidavit and was chagrined that he had been duped and had sworn to something that he no longer believed to be true. Was it Hogan who had convinced him not to cooperate with me? If so, why? Did Hogan not want the details of the bungling of the right to use Dr. Pieroni as a witness to be known? Was Hogan afraid that Kathy might sue him? Was he protecting Susan Loggans and Lee DeWald? Was Hogan not even involved in Dr. Pieroni's abrupt change of mind?

I considered it possible that Dr. Pieroni had nothing to hide but was just embarrassed to meet with me face to face. Because of that possibility I wanted to give him an opportunity to respond to some questions without ever meeting me. Accordingly, I wrote to him once again.

December 27, 1985

Dr. Robert Pieroni
15 Riverdale
Tuscaloosa, Alabama, 35406

Dear Dr. Pieroni:

I was, of course, terribly disappointed to receive your letter stating that you would be unable to get together with me next week. I had looked forward to meeting you and discussing matters of mutual interest. I certainly understand your reservations about a face to face interview with someone you do not know, however. As I mentioned, I am writing a book about this whole ordeal. I intend for the book to be comprehensive, including all aspects of the case. Your affidavit and your willingness to testify against us will certainly be an important part of the book. Of course, I am interested in having all of the book be as accurate and fair as possible. Accordingly, I would appreciate it if you would consider writing to me and clarifying some questions that I have. Again, Dr. Pieroni, I want to reiterate that I bear no malice toward you and have no interest in using the information for any purpose other than literary accuracy. Assuming that you would be willing to assist me in this new format, I have taken the liberty of including the questions that I would appreciate your addressing. I would sincerely appreciate your answering the questions in as much detail as possible. I realize that I am asking for a considerable amount of time and energy. However, I remain convinced that this endeavor might be valuable not only to the two of us, but to many of our fellow physicians as well.

I shall look forward to hearing from you.

Sincerely,

Howard C. Snider, M.D.

I enclosed the following list of questions.

1. Your affidavit states your opinion to be that Kathy received deficient postoperative care. Specifically, what were the deficiencies you identified?

2. The affidavit further states that you believe Kathy had postoperative sepsis. Are you still of this opinion? If so, upon what do you base that opinion?

3. Do you believe Kathy's antibiotics should have been continued past the second postoperative day? If so, would the reason for continuing them be prophylactic or therapeutic?

4. If you believe antibiotics should have been continued for prophylactic reasons, do you have any references to support

continuing antibiotics past 48 hours when a patient has a well drained ureteral repair which is leaking? Any personal experience with the same?

5. If you believe she needed the antibiotics for therapeutic reasons, how do you account for the fact that she progressively defervesced over the next five days after the antibiotics were stopped and was afebrile on the seventh postoperative day?

6. If she was septic, what was the source for it? How do you account for the fact that at laparotomy May 17, she had no evidence of infection in her pelvis? A negative blood culture on May 15? No significant fever May 15?

7. In a similar patient with a normal postoperative temperature curve who is clinically doing well, is there any bacteria which could be cultured from the draining urine which would warrant treatment? If so, do you know of any references which would support that notion?

8. Your affidavit states your opinion to be that Kathy's stroke was caused by sepsis. In the absence of heart disease, is there any pathophysiological mechanism by which pelvic sepsis could cause a cerebrovascular accident? If so, do you have any references to support that opinion? And personal experience?

9. Your affidavit states your opinion is that Kathy lost her leg as a result of sepsis. What was the mechanism involved? If the contention is that pelvic sepsis caused phlebitis, do you have any references to support the notion that sepsis causes *iliofemoral* thrombophlebitis? Any personal experience?

10. If you believe sepsis caused her phlebitis, why do you believe that to be a more likely etiology than the well-recog-

nized etiology of radical pelvic surgery in an obese woman with cancer?

11. Was the development of thrombophlebitis related to the severed ureter? If so, how? How do you account for the fact that the urine leak was in the vicinity of the right iliac vein and her phlebitis was on the left?

12. Are you aware of any alternate explanation other than sepsis which would explain Kathy's abrupt deterioration May 15, a concommitant stroke, and the gradual worsening of her left leg with the resultant gangrene?

13. Your affidavit is dated September 26, 1985 — about a month after our trial. Were you aware of the testimony that took place in the trial when you signed the affidavit?

14. Have you learned anything subsequent to September 26 that has caused you to change the opinions you expressed in the affidavit? If so, I would appreciate your elaboration in as much detail as you are comfortable with.

15. How did you become involved in this case? Were you contacted by Ben Hogan? If so, how did he select you? Have you testified before in malpractice cases, either by deposition or court appearance?

Dr. Pieroni's terse reply the following day made it abundantly clear that he was not going to divulge any information whatsoever. He wrote that he could see no useful purpose to any further discussion of Kathy's case. He reiterated his sentiments from his previous letters and again wished me the best of luck.

Thus ended my brief and less than satisfactory relationship with Dr. Pieroni. I wasn't sure exactly how I wanted him to help, but I felt that he was probably in a unique position to see aspects of our system which were in need of reform. I still prefer to believe he was not a "hired gun" and, if not, I regret that we could not have accomplished something more constructive together. His abrupt change of heart and his reluctance to meet with me remain enigmatic to this day.

Chapter 30

Something is wrong; there needeth a change.
—Robert Browning

Lawyers like to promulgate the notion that, by filing medical malpractice lawsuits, they are contributing to an improvement in the quality of health care delivered in this country. I can see little evidence for any truth in that assertion. In fact, they may well be contributing to the opposite effect.

In the early 1970s when I was a surgical resident, we had weekly "mortality conferences" in which every case of death occurring on the surgical services in the hospital was presented and discussed in detail. The discussions were open and frank. If one of the surgeons thought a patient should have been managed in a different way or that the death could have been prevented, he said so. It was a learning experience where everyone could profit from a retrospective analysis of each case and, if there had been errors in management, hopefully avoid similar problems in the future. The residents called the presentations "yellow sheets" because of our tendency to write all of the details of the case on a yellow legal pad to facilitate presentation of the facts. We lived in perpetual fear of having to present such cases and explain the treatment we had given. It was expected that prior to presenting such a case, the responsible surgeon would have analyzed it thoroughly and identified any deficiencies in care. This process of self analysis and criticism was frequently painful but always beneficial. Every time I made a decision or undertook an intervention in a patient I was caring for, I thought about whether or not I could defend that action in mortality conference if the patient ultimately died. The knowledge that one must stand before his peers and give account of himself is a powerful tool in insuring quality care.

When I entered private practice I was happy to find that all private hospitals also had mortality conferences. They met on a monthly basis rather than a weekly one, and the discussions were perhaps not quite as candid as they had been at academic institutions; nevertheless, we still pointed out to each other instances in which we thought the treatment of a patient could have been altered or improved. Everyone profited from the discussion — most of all, the future patients at the hospitals.

Over the past decade I have watched the gradual weakening of mortality conferences to the point that they have now faded into oblivion. The reason for this demise was largely the fear that the comments made in the conferences might fall into the hands of a plaintiff's attorney and initiate a lawsuit. With the rising tide of lawsuits, physicians became increasingly fearful that their recorded comments in conferences would be subpoenaed or that hospital personnel with access to the meetings or records of the meetings might leak the comments to attorneys. Everyone had heard stories of "moles," or informants, working in hospitals and supplying information to avaricious attorneys for a fee. Whether the problem was really of a large magnitude or whether it was a product of the physicians' paranoia did not really matter. The result was the same. Meaningful mortality conferences ceased to exist.

The legal system has also become an impediment to efforts by the medical profession to discipline itself in other ways. A few years ago the American College of Surgeons incurred legal expenses in excess of two thirds of a million dollars defending a single attempt to discipline one of its members for violating the standards of the organization. The legal system stands ready to file restraint of trade suits anytime members of the medical profession attempt to limit the ability of marginal or incompetent doctors to practice. The growth of the legal profession, and its interference in every aspect of our lives has been bemoaned not only by outsiders, but by leading spokesmen for the profession. The Chief Justice of the United States has declared that "we may all be on our way to a society overrun by hordes of lawyers, hungry as locusts, and brigades of judges in numbers never before contemplated."[6] Laurence H. Silberman, former Deputy Attorney General of the United States, concurred, "The legal process, because of its unbridled growth, has become a cancer which threatens the vitality of our forms of capitalism and democracy."[7]

The inordinate capacity of the legal system to embroil everyone in a morass of chaos discourages physicians from becoming involved in efforts to discipline their own ranks. In effect, the legal system tends to protect the incompetent physicians and interferes with efforts to discipline them.

The medical profession already requires more rigorous training and has higher standards of licensure than any other profession. Unencumbered by legal restraints, efforts to discipline or revoke licenses of incompetent physicians would surely improve. We need laws which encourage physicians to discipline each other without fear of reprisal if they have acted in good faith. More importantly, we need to separate the discipline of errant physicians from the process by which patients are compensated for untoward results of treatment. Somehow we erred long ago when we allowed those two separate issues to become so entwined. Our tendency to handle other misfortunes differently is rooted in antiquity.

Prior to the advent of our modern civilizations, man had little to protect himself from the misfortunes of life which befell him. If he fell prey to a superior beast, an illness, or the like, he was just out of luck. No one was there to share his misfortune or lessen its consequences. As time went on, there came the realization that by banding together in a give and take relationship with his neighbors, he could afford himself at least some protection against the vicissitudes of life. Civilization was born. Part of the philosophy of developing civilizations was the trend for many to pitch in and help the victims of misfortune. If a person's house burned, his neighbors helped him rebuild it. When sickness struck, neighbors would bring food, or help with household chores, or tend to the crops until the person was on his feet again. Gradually there developed the concept of pooling limited resources from many in order to compensate the few who sustain major losses — to "insure" that one's misfortunes will not be devastating. Buying insurance policies of one sort or another has become so commonplace that we now accept it as a natural way of life. We buy life insurance so that, in the event of an untimely death, our families will be protected from financial ruin by receiving a predetermined sum of money which was ultimately derived from many people who did not die at an early age. We buy insurance for our homes, our automobiles, our abilities to earn a living, and even our health, the money for each claim being derived from a great many people whose homes do not burn, who do not have automobile accidents, who continue to earn a living and remain relatively healthy. In some instances the amount of money awarded is fixed in advance; in others we rely on expert "adjusters" to determine the fair allotment according to fairly standard criteria.

It makes little difference whether our house burns because it is struck by lightening, because it has faulty wiring, or because an arsonist (other than ourselves) deliberately sets the blaze. The insurance company pays the same amount to rebuild the house. Whether our automobile is hit by a careful driver who skids on ice, a driver who has driven for too many hours and falls asleep at the wheel, or a driver who is drunk, the insurance company still pays to repair our automobile. We do not have to prove negligence to recover the damages. If a thief breaks into our home and steals our silver or jewelry, our insurance policy pays for our loss. We do not have to prove that the thief was culpable; we need merely show that we have sustained a loss. Quite apart from the

fact that our insurance company compensates us for our
loss, society has a separate system to address the errant ways
of the thief and, in all likelihood, punish him. Although
some would argue that the thief himself should pay for the
damages, we take it for granted that the system, as structured, is reasonable. And well we should. If we were to depend upon a system which required us to be able to appre-
hend the villain and prove the charges against him, most of
our losses would go uncompensated. Even if we were successful in establishing his culpability, the thief's resources
would likely not be adequate to compensate us for our losses.
Thus it is that *we* have insurance to protect *us* from the loss.
The thief does not have insurance to compensate us for our
losses acquired at his hands. So it should be with our health
losses. It is the *patient* who should be insured against any
losses. A separate system entirely should be used to address
the question of the physician's culpability and the disciplinary action, if any, against him.

In sharp contrast to the way we handle other losses, if we
exit from a hospital with a loss which we had not anticipated,
we recover damages from a pooled source of funds *only* if
we can prove we were harmed by negligence. Never mind
the fact that an amputated leg or a stroke is an equally
devastating loss regardless of whether it resulted from negligence, from a conscientious physician's honest error in judgment or technique, or by an act of God. It makes little
sense that we expend enormous sums of money on attorneys,
expert witnesses and the like, debating before an uninformed
jury whether there was negligence and, if so, whether it was
the "proximate cause" of the loss. Depending upon the
abilities of the attorneys and the composition of the jury,
we may walk away with nothing, with a fair and reasonable
compensation, or with a windfall bonanza. It is illogical that

we persist in using a costly, inefficient, haphazard system in which the majority of money spent goes, not to the victims of the misfortune, but the ancillary people in the scheme — the lawyers, expert witnesses, and the like.

These inequities will persist as long as we use an adversarial system to settle issues which should rightly be relegated to an inquisitive one. In an adversarial system, neither side seeks to find truth or to be fair; both strive to win. Tort reform will not solve the problem. It will only change the inequity equation such that one side is temporarily at a greater advantage and the other at a disadvantage. The inequity of the system will persist.

One who seriously examines the situation cannot help wondering why we do not handle the victims of "bad medical results" the same way we handle the victims of house fires, untimely deaths, disabilities, and automobile accidents. Compensate the victim in a rational, equitable manner, regardless of the cause, and address the question of disciplining a possible offender as a separate matter through a separate system entirely. Society, of course, would have to decide how charitable the system would be to the victims of misfortune, both in terms of the definition of a compensable result, and the amount of compensation for each one. If all "bad medical results" were compensated, the cost of the system would be enormous. If only catastrophic ones were compensated, the cost would be minimal, but individuals would have to accept the chance that they would be victims of moderately bad results without compensation, somewhat analogous to a "deductible" clause in an insurance policy. The cost of the system would, as always, be borne by the members of society regardless of the mechanism of distribution.

Such a sytem would be very much in line with how we

insure ourselves against other misfortunes. If all of the money currently paid in malpractice premiums and only a small portion of the money currently used for "defensive medicine" were available for distribution to unfortunate patients, far more of them would get equitable settlements than do so today. And they would get the money without their doctor viewing them as an adversary. Obviously, the amounts of compensation settled upon by society would not be adequate in all instances. A person who earns large sums of money before sustaining an imperfect result which precludes that continued earning may not be adequately compensated by the societal formula. That person could have the option of purchasing "additional coverage," much like one would purchase additional flight insurance before getting on an airplane.

There would surely be problems involved in defining what constituted a result bad enough to be compensated and in deciding whether individual cases fell within the criteria. We have precedents, however, that suggest such a system would be workable. For years, disability determination boards have taken the results of examinations provided to them by unbiased physicians and arrived at reasonably fair allocations according to certain rather clearly proscribed criteria. Workmen's compensation claims are handled in a similar manner. The physician is not an adversary but, if not a friend, at least an impartial provider of unbiased facts. The weighers of the facts are people trained in applying them in a rational and equitable manner to the applicable criteria. They make the determinations on a daily basis in a relatively uniform manner. Surely they are more capable of achieving equitable results than a haphazardly selected group of people who perhaps decide one case in a lifetime.

Would there be problems in such a system? Of course.

But it is difficult to imagine its being less equitable and less fair than our current one. Even if we elect to continue to compensate recipients of bad results based only upon whether there has been negligence involved, everyone (except attorneys) would profit if that determination were done in a rational manner by a panel of professionals.

Rep. Robert Mrazek of New York wrote, "The more I research the malpractice issue, the more I am convinced that the fundamentally adversarial nature of our judicial system is simply not the best way to resolve the many complex aspects of medical liability. Truly effective reform will require, in my view, an alternative to the judicial system." He has introduced legislation which would set up an alternative to our present way of handling claims of malpractice. According to his plan, panels would be established under the direction of the attorneys general of each state to hear claims of malpractice. These panels would consist of a medical professional, a lawyer, and a layperson, along with others as appointed by the attorney general. They would not serve in a screening role, sending those cases with merit on to the judicial system for trial. Rather, they would be empowered to render a judgment and dispense with the case permanently.

Defense attorneys maintain that a panel of experts would rule in favor of the plaintiff far more often than a jury would. So be it. I do not want to remain in the position in which I have to hope my patients who have sustained serious losses are not compensated for them. I also do not want to be portrayed as incredibly callous, uncaring, and negligent in order for them to collect that compensation. A major change in the system would benefit almost everyone. We need to get on with it.

John Cameron retired two months after our trial — a

direct result of the strain imposed by the lawsuit. Had it not been for the suit, I am certain he would still be practicing today. He left an unfillable void where he had been. He loved to perform surgery and to care for sick people, but he could not afford to risk losing the security he had worked his entire life to obtain. The group was just not the same without him, and I sorely missed his presence in it. One year later I left it and established a solo practice.

Since our trial ended I have evaluated on a daily basis the pressure and tension under which I practice, getting ever closer to the point that I, too, can no longer persevere. The sleepless nights did not cease with the ending of the trial. Not only do I continue to agonize over each critically ill patient the same way I always have — the way Dr. Kirklin must have sensed fifteen years earlier — but I have begun to view each one as a potential adversary in a court of law. Every time I take a vacation or a weekend off, leaving a sick patient in the care of someone else, I wonder if someone will one day again accuse me of 'jumping ship.'' The knowledge that there are 1,200 medical malpractice cases pending against Alabama's 3,000 physicians makes it intuitively obvious that, if I continue to care for high risk patients as I have been, my time will soon come again.

I am forty-four years old, presumably in my prime, with perhaps another good twenty years to practice. I do not want to give up something that I dearly love and have devoted so much of myself to. The point may come, though, where giving it up is mandatory for my survival and happiness. I cling to the hope that the change which is so desperately needed in our system will not be long in coming.

1.   Lawrence M. Friedman, *A History of American Law* (New York: Simon & Schuster, 1973), p. 95.

2.   Bruce G. Sebille, "Trial by Jury: an Ineffective Survival, *ABAJ* 10 (1924), 53, 55.

3.   Jerome Frank, *Courts on Trial* (Princeton: Princeton University Press, 1949), p. 132.

4.   Leon Sarky, "Civil Juries, Their Decline and Eventual Fall," *Loyola Law Review*, 11 (1962-53), 243-245.

5.   Erwin Nathaniel Griswold, "Dean's Report," Harvard Law School, 1962-1963, pp. 5-6.

6.   *Time,* April 10, 1978, p. 56.

7.   Laurence H. Silberman, Regulation, March/April, 1978, p. 15.

Afterword

It has been three years since our trial ended and about a year since I finished, except for minor revisions, the manuscript for this book. My thoughts and my feelings are still largely the same as I have recorded them. Time has perhaps dulled the intensity somewhat, but the same pain is still there. There are sections of this book that I still cannot read without extreme distress. The words and the emotions which accompanied them are probably forever interconnected in my brain. As time goes by, though, I become more convinced that, despite the pain physicians feel when charged with negligence, they are not the ones who suffer the most as a result of our system: patients are.

There seems to be a glimmer of hope on the horizon, though. Unbeknown to me, while I was writing this book, the American Medical Association and thirty-one medical specialty societies were working on a proposal for an alternative system for resolving professional liability claims. In January, 1988, their proposal for a fault-based administrative system to replace our current one was issued. The well-researched proposal addresses essentially all of the major problems I have raised in this book and offers a comprehensive solution for most of them. The report cites evidence that currently less than five percent of patients who suffer as a result of malpractice receive any compensation whatsoever. It offers the potential for correcting that problem by providing all patients access to the system, an expeditious hearing, and a rational, uniform settlement outside of the jury system. There are also provisions for more rigorous credentialing of physicians and more effective performance monitoring and disciplinary actions.

Although it is merely a proposal at this point, I hope that it is the beginning of true medical liability reform.